God and Caesar
on the
Potomac

A Pilgrimage of Conscience

Other Books by Robert F. Drinan, S.J.

Religion, the Courts and Public Policy, 1963
Democracy, Dissent & Disorder, 1969
Vietnam and Armageddon, 1970
The Right to Be Educated (editor), 1968
Honor the Promise—America's Commitment to Israel, 1977
Beyond the Nuclear Freeze, 1983

God and Caesar on the Potomac

A Pilgrimage of Conscience

Writings and Addresses
on
Justice and Peace

Robert F. Drinan, S.J.

Preface by
Jimmy Carter,
Former President of the United States

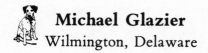

Michael Glazier
Wilmington, Delaware

Acknowledgements
The Publisher wishes to acknowledge and thank the following for use of material in this book: *National Catholic Reporter, America Press, The New Catholic World, The New York Times, The Christian Century,* and the *Boston Herald American.*

First published in 1985 by Michael Glazier, Inc., 1723 Delaware Avenue, Wilmington, Delaware, 19806 • ©1985 by Robert F. Drinan, S.J. All rights reserved. • Library of Congress Card Catalog Number: 84-48454 • International Standard Book Number: 0-89453-450-5 • Cover design by Brother Placid, O.S.B. • Printed in the United States of America

Contents

IV
Civil Rights

Part V
The Equal Rights Amendment

Part VI
The Death Penalty

Part VII
The Poor

Part VIII
Soviet Jews/Israel

Appendixes
The Impeachment of President Nixon

Preface

Father Drinan's credentials as a humanitarian, religious leader, and thinker are unassailable. He is a direct descendant and torch-bearer of the most prominent Jesuit leaders in the history of the Catholic Church.

In the polarized politics of the 1980's some religious leaders have come under increasing fire for invoking their religious values to justify various public policies in the political arena. Yet no such criticism can be accurately leveled against Robert Drinan. While he is truly a man of God, a man of deep principle, and a man of profound conscience, his astute grasp of practical solutions to world problems enables him to debate policy as a scholar and practitioner, as well as a religious leader.

Rather, he has made the broad ethical precepts of his Jesuit upbringing — peace among peoples, justice and charity, human rights, dignity for the poor and disadvantaged — an integral part of his public actions.

It is his commitment to apply his religious views of human dignity to life's bitter realities that make Father Drinan a recognized leader against any denial of individual freedoms —at home or abroad, by governments or by individuals.

But conscience alone does not dictate Father Drinan's appeals. Pragmatism — a sense of what can actually be accomplished in a real-life framework — plays a large role as well. With a deep-rooted commitment to the preservation of humankind, for example, he has repeatedly appealed to Americans to join the nuclear freeze movement and to reverse the threatening nuclear spiral. Yet, acknowledging the illusory approach to demanding total abolition of nuclear weapons, he urges a realistic solution to one of the great moral and ethical issues of our age, preventing nuclear holocaust. This is typical of Father Drinan's unique ability to find practical solutions, premised on ethical values, to complex issues.

In a similar vein, Father Drinan has brought the full thrust of his religious heritage to bear against political persecution around the globe. Exploring human rights abuses in Latin America, he asks all of us to search for what is just, not only for Americans, but for all mankind. Criticizing the imbalanced human rights policies of the Reagan Administration, he speaks for all the world's oppressed in asking for even-handed application of human rights by the Administration.

Father Drinan assails other infringements of peace and social justice. He advances the cause of women's rights; he speaks for the poor and the homeless; he challenges capital punishment.

Father Drinan's writings, like his life, are a mixture of religion and politics. He has successfully struck the difficult balance of a deeply religious person, who applies his religious principles in the sphere of political life without imposing his religious creed on others.

To Father Drinan, social and economic justice are inseparable from the basic tenets of his religion and the mission of the Society of Jesus.

This collection is a unique exploration of social conscience. It makes important points for us all without sermonizing. These writings underscore the constructive role which religious principles can play in world politics. As in the active and involved life he leads each day, Father Drinan speaks about the good in mankind for the good of mankind.

I am proud to know Father Drinan as a religious scholar and thinker blending time-honored principles with modern realities; as a man of action in the United States Congress, fighting for peace and social justice; and as a friend and human being of profound integrity, honesty, and sensitivity to his fellow men and women. This book is a fitting testament to his life and to his work.

Jimmy Carter,
Former President of the United States

Introduction

When it was first proposed that a collection of my writings and addresses be issued as a volume, I was unenthused by the idea. I felt that such a collection would not constitute a coherent body of thought related to one of the principal objectives of my life — the advancement of the church's goals in the realm of peace and justice. But on reflection I realize that seldom if ever can anyone put out a definitive statement on any of the great moral or social issues of the day. Events and issues are fast moving and become more complicated as they unfold. Consequently, one must try to seize each teachable moment when a reassertion or a reillumination of the principles of peace and justice applied to a particular situation will be heard. I have the hope, therefore, that the writings in this volume will reflect some of the struggles for peace and justice with which the Catholic church and all religious bodies are now engaged.

Work on behalf of social justice and peace among nations has, of course, always been the work of the church. There is abundant evidence to demonstrate that the positions on moral and social issues taken by the church through the centuries have helped advance civilization and elevate the standards of human conduct. But in modern times the church has felt a special need to direct its attention to the undeniable moral and spiritual issues involved in capitalism, colonialism, and nationalism.

At least since 1891 with the publication by Pope Leo XIII's encyclical *Rerum Novarum* the church has taken firm positions on the major moral questions which underlie the functioning of capitalism in the modern world. Pope Leo's basic approaches to the problem of management and labor in a capitalistic system were re-enunciated and clarified 40 years later by Pope Pius XI in *Quadragesimo Anno.*

Jesuits have always taken a deep and special interest in the work of clarifying and implementing the social teachings of the church. Jesuits with their schools and publications are obviously in a position to make known the doctrine of the Holy See. From my earliest days as a Jesuit the constant efforts of the Society of Jesus to carry out this task were everywhere visible. They took many forms — institutes for members of labor unions, schools for future lawyers and businessmen, retreats for professional people and any number of similar apostolates.

This mission to educate the world in the social doctrines of the church was ratified, confirmed and expanded by the Second Vatican Council. The ringing exhortations of the major documents of Vatican II have become the marching orders of Jesuits and millions of others around the world. Catholicism, of course, was not changed by Vatican II. But it was enriched, enlarged, made more beautiful and proclaimed as a religion which, along with the Gospel and because of the Gospel, teaches that the attainment of social justice is a basic and essential part of the message and mission of the Catholic church.

The most dramatic flowering of the social teachings of Vatican II came in Latin America where the bishops, meeting at Medellin, a city in Colombia, in 1968, proclaimed that the church in Latin America would work against the "institutionalized violence" present in the continent's economic situation. In addition the bishops said that the church would exercise a "preferential option" for the poor. This approach — startling to some but long awaited by others — was clarified and confirmed by another meeting of the Latin American bishops in Puebla, Mexico, in 1979. These pronouncements were in essence confirmed by Pope John Paul II in his addresses at and after Puebla.

Just before Medellin and Puebla Pope Paul VI emphatically affirmed the social teachings of the church in the encyclical *Populorum Progressio* issued in 1967.

The modern evolution of the church's social teachings has been chronicled in a splendid volume by Father Donald Dorr, *Option for the Poor: A Hundred Years of Vatican Social Teaching* (Gill and MacMillan, Orbis, 1983). Father Dorr writes of the establishment in 1967 by Pope Paul VI of the Pontifical Commission for Justice and Peace and the influence this group had on the document, *Justice in the World*, issued late in 1971 by the Synod of Bishops. He also demonstrates the comprehensiveness and the continuity of the social teaching of the church from 1891 to the publication in 1981 of *Laborem Exercens* On Human Works to commemorate the 90th anniversary of *Rerum Novarum*. That body of teaching makes the church and some 800 million Catholics a dynamic force for change in the social order. As one rereads the documents from popes, from synods of bishops and from the hierarchies of the world, one is amazed at the profound and pervasive devotion to social and economic justice which is a constitutive part of contemporary Catholicism.

The highest authorities of the Jesuit order have on three solemn occasions echoed the call of the Holy See for the attainment of social justice. Seeking to integrate the directives of Vatican II into the mission of the Jesuit order the 31st General Congregation of the Society of Jesus, meeting in 1965 and 1966, made it clear that work for justice must go hand in hand with works and writings explaining the Catholic faith. Work on behalf of faith and justice are indivisible elements of the same apostolate. The millions of men and women who witness bitter injustice in their daily lives cannot be expected to have faith in a just God. The directives for Jesuits to engage in social action were specific and almost imperious. The 300 Jesuits at the 31st General Congregation spelled out their conclusions and their commands in these words:

1. The social apostolate is fully in harmony with the apostolic end of the Society of Jesus....

2. The social apostolate strives directly by every endeavor to build a fuller expression of justice and charity into the structures of human life in common.

3. The "humanization" of social life...is particularly effective as a way of bearing evangelical witness in our time.

4. The Society of Jesus can contribute to the social apostolate of the church by "establishing the presence of the church in the great national and international associations and congresses that attempt to bring about such progress."

The sweep and scope of the 31st General Congregation of the Jesuit order was global; it noted how "people are troubled not only about their wages ... working conditions...and social security but are especially concerned with the massive world-wide problems of malnutrition, illiteracy, unemployment [and] overpopulation." And it is to all of these problems that the attention of Jesuits is directed.

A decade after this exhortation to work for social justice the 32nd General Congregation of the Jesuits was even more clear and more compelling in its mandate that Jesuits work simultaneously for the service of faith and the promotion of justice.

The second paragraph of the lengthy statement issued in 1975 by the 32nd General Congregation affirms the linking of faith and justice in these strong words:

> The mission of the Society of Jesus today is the service of faith, of which the promotion of justice is an absolute requirement. For reconciliation with God demands the reconciliation of people with one another.

The General Congregation later refers to the "simple, steady aim of the service of faith and the promotion of justice." As a result Jesuits should be ready "not only to recognize the rights of all, especially the poor and the powerless, but also to work actively to secure those rights." This directive is of divine origin because "the promotion of justice is an integral part of the priestly service of the faith."

The document urges Jesuits to work against "an aura of legitimacy" given to "unjust social structures" by "certain false images of God." This work is necessary because now it is "within human power to make the world more just." Consequently, Jesuits must recognize that the "injustice that racks our world in so many forms is, in fact, a denial of God in practice, for it denies the dignity of the human person, the image of God, the brother or sister of Christ."

The social involvement required of Jesuits is spelled out in these words:

> Our faith in Christ Jesus and our mission to proclaim the Gospel demand of us a commitment to promote justice and to enter into solidarity with the voiceless and the powerless. This commitment will move us seriously to verse ourselves in the complex problems which they face in their lives, then to identify and assume our own responsibilities to society.

Finally the General Congregation states bluntly that the "promotion of justice is not *one* apostolic area among others ...rather it should be the concern of our whole life and the dimension of all our apostolic endeavors."

In order to leave no doubt about the centrality of the linking of faith and justice the General Congregation sums up the Jesuit mission in these words:

> To promote justice, to proclaim the faith and to lead others to a personal encounter with Christ are the three inseparable elements that make up the whole of our apostolate.

In 1983 the 33rd General Congregation of the Society of Jesus reaffirmed the commitment of the Jesuit order to the "service of faith of which the promotion of justice is an absolute requirement." Jesuits are to be deeply concerned about all kinds of social injustice and are required to work for the "promotion of a more just world order" and to strive for "international justice and an end of the arms race that deprives the poor and threatens to destroy civilization."

Since the 33rd General Congregation came together principally to elect a new general rather than to rethink the basic guidelines of the Jesuit apostolate in the modern world, the decrees of the congregation are relatively brief. But it is clear that the inseparable role of the service of faith and the promotion of justice was endorsed anew.

I have dealt somewhat at length with the ecclesiastical and Jesuit directives to associate the service of faith with the promotion of justice. I have done so because the linking of faith and justice has been central to all that I have done and have written.

Ever since my ordination to the priesthood in 1953, I have been intensely aware of the essential part which social justice should and does have in my apostolate. In my teaching of law, in my writings and addresses, issues related to economic, social and political justice have been paramount.

I have also sought to present substantial treatments of issues related to social justice in my five books. I mention these volumes simply to point out that the writings in this present collection are not contained in these books. In 1963 I published *Religion, the Courts and Public Policy* (McGraw Hill) — a discussion of the major church-state issues in the United States from the viewpoint of Catholic teaching. In 1969, as students and others from Berlin to Berkeley demonstrated, I published *Democracy, Dissent and Disorder* (Seabury) — an analysis of the rights and duties of those who were not prepared to wait for the correction of social injustices by the ordinary political processes. In 1970, after visiting Vietnam on a human rights mission with a group of churchmen, I published *Vietnam and Armageddon* (Sheed and Ward) — an application of the Catholic church's position on war as set forth in Vatican II to the situation in Vietnam. In 1977 I published a volume, *Honor the Promise* (Doubleday), with my reflections on Christian-Jewish relations with particular reference to Israel. In 1983 I wrote about what is probably the greatest moral and political issue facing civilization — nuclear war. In *Beyond the Nuclear Freeze* (Seabury) I analyzed the pastoral of the American hierarchy on nuclear war and applied its principles and approach to the struggle for nuclear arms control as manifested in the movement for a mutual and verifiable nuclear freeze.

Although some of these themes are touched in the writings collected in this volume, the essays here are more in the nature of responses to a wide variety of issues related to peace and social justice. They represent attempts to apply the basic principles of Catholic theology to particular situations. They frequently seek to evolve a legal remedy for a moral or social problem. If this collection does nothing more than demonstrate the urgency with which the church seeks to enlarge social justice in the modern world, its publication may not have been in vain.

PART I

International
Human Rights

Chapter 1

Reflections on Latin America and Human Rights

At turning points in our life, we look to discern ways in which the Holy Spirit may be speaking to us. Today we have to be overwhelmed at the extent and the growth in the evils and errors which we see everywhere in the world. It is a global village raging with madness. There are 50,000 nuclear weapons in existence with 30,000 of them in the possession of the United States; we are in addition constructing three more nuclear weapons each day — 1,300 each year. Simultaneously we see 800 million people chronically malnourished with every third child in the Third World dying before the age of five.

Do we have to live with this potential holocaust all our lives? What does God intend for us since by his providence we live amid this co-existence in terror — a scourge never known to humanity before? We are weary of protesting the unbelievable arms race — the $525 billion which mankind spends each year on arms — more than $1 billion a day — and we look for some sign as to how we should think, pray or act. Signs are few but let me speak to two areas where perhaps God is speaking to us — (1) the persecutions and martyrdoms in Latin America, and (2) the remarkable convergence of the sacred and the secular in the area of human rights.

Commencement Address at Weston School of Theology, May 23, 1981.

3

*Martyrdom: The Fate of Those Who Believe in the
Liberation of Latin America*

A short time before his martyrdom, Archbishop Romero
uttered these prophetic words:

> Our persecutors are confused. They are not used to seeing
> the face of a church converted to the poor . . . That is why
> they have no other category for us but that of subversives.
> And they treat us in the only way they know how: with
> violent words and violent actions. . . .

There is some hope that the several martyrdoms in El Salvador, the persecution of the church in Guatemala and the collaboration of Catholics and Communists in the successful
revolution against Saomoza in Nicaragua have finally aroused
the church in the United States to the dreadful economic and
political repression in Latin America where one-half of the
members of the Catholic church reside. There have been many,
many signs from Latin America over a long period of time to
reveal to us the plight of our companions in Christ on that
continent. But the warnings in Medellin in 1969, the pleas of
Puebla a decade later and the emergence of liberation theology
did not arouse us to use our influence to remove the political
and corporate support of the United States from the oligar-
chies, the dictatorships and the military governments which
oppress 350 million Catholics in virtually every nation of Latin
America.

God has finally resorted to martyrdoms in order to shock us
into some sense of the complicity of American power and
arrogance with that network which, in the name of capitalism
and national security restricts religious freedom, denies the
right to democratic elections and deprives millions of campesi-
nos of any right to the land which they till.

Despite the unwillingness or inability of American Catholics
to hear, we should rejoice that the church in Latin America has
become probably the one institution that may now have the
capacity to liberate the people from servitude to that traditional triumvirate of oligarchy — army — church which has
effectively deprived the people of Latin America of those rights

to which they are entitled both by reason of their creation and by reason of international law. And that is why — in the words noted above of Archbishop Romero — the established powers "have no other category for us but subversives." It follows that those who believe in the liberation advocated by the Second Vatican Council, by Medellin, by Puebla and by Pope John Paul II in Brazil, will be treated, again in the words of Archbishop Romero, in the only way they know how: "with violent words and violent actions."

We can expect continued "violent words and violent actions" by those in power in Latin America against priests, nuns and anyone who urges social and economic change. We may even have to expect verbal abuse from the State Department directed against Catholic missionaries in Latin America who will tell their fellow believers that they have a right to demand equality before the law and the right to participate in the government which rules their lives.

The "violent words and violent actions," predicted by Archbishop Romero will be forthcoming in an aggravated way against those in Latin America who urged collaboration with socialists and Marxists. It is not very enlightened for Catholics in North America to adopt a doctrinaire position that Marxist principles can never be useful or appropriate in Latin America or in the Third World. Catholics will be required, furthermore, to argue persuasively against the simplistic view of the administration in Washington that the insurgencies in South America are the result of Cuban or communist infiltration into groups of unsuspecting peasants.

What we must never forget is that the very severe criticism of capitalism set forth by the 350 bishops of Latin America at Puebla; we must also recall the grave charges brought against capitalism by Pope John Paul II in Brazil. Here are his words:

> The persistency of injustice threatens the existence of society within. This menace from within really exists when the distribution of goods is grounded only in the economic laws of growth and a bigger profit....

Everywhere around us the assumption is that if free enterprise and the multinational corporations are permitted to operate without restraint in Latin America, economic justice will soon prevail. This glorification of capitalism is totally opposed to the encyclicals and all of Catholic social tradition.

In a recently published statement of Father Pedro Arrupe, the Jesuit General, on the use of "marxist analysis" it is significant that he wants textbooks scrutinized lest they inculcate the view of capitalism which, in Father Arrupe's words is: "an individualistic and materialistic vision of life that is destructive of Christian values and attitudes."

The presence of martyrs in Latin America is the most recent and most dramatic call to our conscience to assist our co-believers in all of the tormented countries of South America. We have unwittingly participated in their enslavement. Let us resolve that after today we will as never before listen to the Holy Spirit and follow what we are so clearly being asked to do: to liberate a continent from the torment and the turmoil of a selfish capitalistic economy aided by governments that brutally use military power to institutionalize their tyranny.

Human Rights: The Dominant Moral Idea of This Generation

There exists today a most remarkable convergence of a sacred and a secular emphasis on human rights. In Brazil in 1980, Pope John Paul II spoke of human rights more than any other idea. It is also significant to note that in the years 1974 to 1980 the United States had what might come to be called the golden age of emphasizing human rights as an essential part of our foreign policy. During that period, the Congress enacted legislation which would deny economic and military assistance to those nations which are guilty of a "persistent pattern of gross violations of internationally guaranteed human rights." During the past several years, aid has been denied to countries like Guatemala, Argentina, Uraguay and others because of their deplorable record on human rights. It is overwhelmingly clear that hundreds, even thousands, of persons have been freed from prison and that democratic elections have been held because nations respected or feared the human rights policy of the American government.

It is still tragic, however, that, according to Amnesty International, torture still exists in some 40 nations. In addition, there are 17,000 political prisoners in South America, with 30,000 additional people missing.

This idea of emphasizing human rights derives of course from the adoption of the United Nations charter where in articles 55 and 56 this nation along with all signatories of the United Nations charter made a "pledge" to "promote" human rights.

Despite that pledge, the United States has ratified only five of the least controversial of the 19 treaties which have emerged from the United Nations.

In 1975, the Thirty-Second General Congregation of the Jesuit Order stated that the mission of the Society of Jesus today "demands a life in which the justice of the gospel shines out in a willingness not only to recognize and respect the rights of all, especially the poor and the powerless, but also to work actively to secure those rights." The same General Congregation put it more graphically with these words:

> There are millions of men and women in our world — specific people with names and faces — who are suffering from poverty and hunger, from the unjust distribution of wealth and resources and from the consequences of racial, social, and political discrimination.

It would seem clear that the Holy Spirit is telling us that we should join with the entire world in emphasizing human rights as an essential part of our spirituality, the approach of the Catholic church and the foreign policy of our nation. It will be relatively easy to applaud the emphasis on human rights which appears everywhere. But it will be difficult to press forward in realistic ways to make our devotion to human rights, both as Christians and as citizens, a reality in the world.

It will be possible for us to implement human rights only if we remind ourselves regularly of what Father Pierre Teilhard de Chardin said when he wrote that "my chief interest in life has been a general attempt to find God more easily in the world. It is the only vocation I know as my own, and nothing can turn me from it." Teilhard said it well in another context when he wrote that "our faith imposes on us the right and the duty to throw ourselves into the things of the earth."

As all of us face the agonies which mankind will undergo in the next 20 years we must recognize that one of our greatest temptations will be the desire to escape from the world. We will rationalize this desire and claim that it is the Holy Spirit who is telling us to shun the secular, avoid the temporal, and withdraw into the safety of a personalized religion. We may even try to withdraw from the world in the name of living as a Christian. But the shattering truth is that we run away from God if we run away from the world. We lose sight of the Deity when we take our eyes off God's cosmic reflections in the world.

We know that the martyrdoms in Latin America and the persecution of the church in so many countries of the continent speak to us in dramatic ways of what we should be doing personally and collectively to liberate the people and the church in South America. At the same time, we see the majesty of human rights presented to us along with a most remarkable consensus of church and state, of government and religion. Perhaps it is time to rejoice that the ideas of liberation and human rights, so central to Christianity, are now the aspiration and dream of America as a nation. But we know that we as people of faith and as citizens of America are unique and that we have a mission and destiny not given to others. Archibald MacLeish put it well in these words:

> There are those who will say that the liberation of mankind, the freedom of man and mind, is nothing but a dream. They are right. It is the American dream.

Chapter 2

Amnesty Work Grows in Urgency

It is exhilarating but exhausting to read the 426-page annual report of Amnesty International issued December 9, 1981. It is exhilarating because the 250,000 members of Amnesty International in more than 150 countries really care. But it is exhausting because one sees that sickening repetition of torture, illegal detention and political executions which Amnesty International has monitored so effectively since it was established in 1961.

Amnesty International makes no assessment as to whether repression is increasing. It expresses only the conviction that the awareness of repression is growing because, among other factors, it is "now harder for states to hide repression."

Amnesty is scrupulously nonpolitical and nonpartisan, but it is clearly directing its remarks at the Reagan administration when it states that it is "dismayed by a tendency among governments to regard certain abuses as more acceptable when committed by friends than by enemies."

This statement is referring implicitly to the assertion of U.S. Ambassador Jeane Kirkpatrick at the United Nations that the United States must get along with "moderately repressive" governments. Amnesty, on the other hand, asserts boldly that all nations "must be willing to confront political imprisonment, torture and executions wherever they occur."

Amnesty records that in 1981 it was working on behalf of 4,517 individual prisoners of conscience in 64 countries. Thou-

First published in the *National Catholic Reporter*, December 12, 1982.

sands of letters were written to and about these prisons "adopted" by Amnesty. This organization claims no credit if some of them have been released because "seldom does Amnesty International show a direct link between its work and the desired results." But in an extraordinarily moving statement Amnesty describes the results of its work in these words:

> But prisoners do emerge after years of solitary confinement, having read not one letter out of the hundreds sent by groups, yet insisting that they knew of these worldwide efforts, that they knew their families were supported and, above all, that they shared that most human of qualities, hope. Many say that it was hope alone that gave them strength to face another indistinguishable, unnumbered day; to withstand the certainty of more torture to come; to stay sane as the date of execution approached; to cope with imagining the suffering of those they loved.

The brutalities chronicled in Amnesty International's report numb the mind. It is distressing to read of mass executions in Iraq, detention without trial in Zaire and the sentencing to death of 1,295 persons in 41 nations. But it is particularly excruciating to read of the systematic and unspeakably cruel practices that continue in Catholic Latin America. One keeps wondering — can't Catholic officials do *something* to prevent the spectacle and the scandal of nations that contain one-half of the Catholics in the world from indulging in practices condemned by the laws of their own countries, by their church and by the fundamental moral norms of humanity?

Hopeful developments are sparse in Amnesty International's 1981 report. But 4,000 physicians in 26 nations last year wrote to prisoners in ill health, studied the after effects of torture and helped rehabilitate its victims.

Some positive developments occurred in the past year with regard to the abolition of capital punishment. As of April 1981, 23 nations had completely abolished the death penalty and 17 had abolished it for ordinary crimes. The record of the United States, moreover, was outstanding. Although in April 1981, 794 people were under sentence of death in the United States, there are no political prisoners in the technical sense of that word.

The massive documentation in the 1981 report of Amnesty International stands as a living indictment of the cruelty governments continue to inflict on their own citizens. Amnesty International is undoubtedly one of the principal reasons why the very concept of international human rights is now one of the key moral concepts on which, in contemporary society, there is a profound consensus among sacred and secular individuals and organizations.

The report concedes that people are more affected by a "murder in the next street ... than a massacre abroad," but Amnesty International will continue to insist "on the principle of international responsibility for the protection of human rights."

With the silence about and the de-emphasis on human rights in the Reagan administration, the message and mission of Amnesty International are more important than ever before.

Chapter 3

Human Rights and the Reagan Administration

After months of confusion and contradiction the Reagan administration stated in November 1981 that the promotion of human rights would be central to U.S. foreign policy. The White House, however, has little to point to as human rights victories in its first two years. The record demonstrates that the administration's prime preoccupation in the field of human rights is with nations deemed to be friendly to the Soviet Union and unfriendly to the United States. As a result, public criticism of our "friends" on human rights grounds is thought by the administration to weaken their relationship to us.

The Reagan administration takes no position on the five major human rights treaties that have been signed by previous presidents but not ratified by the Senate. Indeed, this is the first administration in history that has not publicly supported U.S. ratification of the Genocide Convention signed by President Truman in 1948.

This approach is a sharp reversal of the law and the practices that made the years 1974 to 1980 the "golden age" of human rights. A law signed by President Ford bans economic and military assistance to countries that engage in a pattern of gross violations of basic human rights. Another law signed by President Carter requires that U.S. representatives to six multilateral development banks channel assistance only to those nations without a consistent pattern of gross violations of human rights.

First published in *America*, March 5, 1983.

Other laws forbid U.S. aid to any nation for internal law enforcement purposes, while legislation passed in 1981 and signed by President Reagan stipulates that aid to Argentina, Chile, El Salvador and Nicaragua is now contingent on presidential certification to Congress that specific human rights standards have been fulfilled.

The record of compliance with these laws by the Reagan administration is dismal. Reviewing its position on human rights in several nations, one has to reach the sad conclusion that the adamant anti-Soviet posture of representatives of the administration has blinded them to the very important value of placing a special emphasis on human rights in U.S. foreign policy.

The repudiation by the administration of a firm accent on human rights has been particularly visible in Latin America. In 1978 Congress banned all military assistance and arms sales to Argentina. The Reagan administration successfully sought repeal of this law, but Congress added a requirement that, prior to giving military aid, the president must certify significant improvements in human rights. The certification must consider whether there has been an accounting for the "disappeared" and whether there has been a release of prisoners held without charges.

As of early January 1983 the Reagan administration had not certified that Argentina qualifies for aid, but the White House says that its failure to certify is not related to the human rights situation. The certification is expected any day, but the recent discovery of more than a thousand corpses of the "disappeared" along with new closings of periodicals and new disappearances may further postpone the date of the certification.

The Reagan administration also reversed previous U.S. practice on multilateral bank loans. It voted in July 1981 in favor of $310 million in such loans for Argentina, although the law forbids such votes in favor of nations that are gross and consistent abusers of human rights. The willingness of the Reagan administration to overlook human rights violations in Argentina was demonstrated in other ways. In 1981 the Administration agreed to a compromise arrangement that reduced the effectiveness of a group authorized by the United Nations

Human Rights commission to investigate the status of the "disappeared" in Argentina. The White House received Argentine Presidents Viola and Galtieri on official visits to Washington. United Nations Ambassador Jeane Kirkpatrick traveled to Buenos Aires to proclaim U.S. friendship but declined to meet with human rights groups.

In December 1981 Congress enacted a requirement that military assistance and arms sales to Chile could be resumed only if the president certified that there had been a "significant improvement" in human rights in Chile and that progress had been made in bringing to justice those indicted by a federal grand jury for the 1976 murders in Washington of Orlando Letelier and Ronni Moffitt. The Reagan administration has not tried to certify that either of these conditions has been met. This is a position for which the Reagan administration should be praised, but this strong human rights stand is undercut by its reversal of previous policy by voting in favor of $126 million in multilateral development bank loans to Chile. There are strong forces within the State Department that want to certify that Chile should receive U.S. aid. If this opinion prevails and the government of General Pinochet receives aid, it will be hard to discern any minimal standard on human rights compliance being observed by the Reagan administration.

In late January 1983 the Reagan administration once again certified that improvements in the human rights situation in El Salvador merited continued military aid. In December 1982, following a meeting with President Magaña of El Salvador, President Reagan stated that he had already made up his mind and that he intended to certify El Salvador once again. All of the groups that monitor human rights in Latin America have denied sharply that the situation has improved in El Salvador. No real progress has been made in the case of the four murdered U.S. churchwomen, since the arrest of the five low-ranking national guardsmen does not resolve the question of the culpability of officers involved in the killings or the cover-up.

More perhaps than in any other country, the commitment of the Reagan administration to maintain the current government in power in El Salvador and to help it in securing a military victory over rebel forces brings about the setting aside of any consideration of human rights. This total abandonment of even lip service to human rights in El Salvador inevitably weakens American credibility elsewhere with respect to human rights.

The Reagan administration has been intensely interested in restoring military assistance and arms sales to Guatemala. This aid was terminated in 1977 because of Guatemala's horrendous record on human rights. In 1981 the White House evaded this prohibition by selling $3.2 million in trucks and jeeps to Guatemala, alleging that these vehicles did not amount to security assistance.

The administration claims that there has been an improvement in human rights since the coup of March 23, 1982, that brought General Efrain Rios Montt to power. Even if this is true in Guatemala City, the slaughter of Guatemalans goes on in the countryside. In December 1982 President Reagan met with President Rios Montt and informed the press that Guatemala was getting a "bum rap" on human rights. The White House has announced that it will support an $18 million loan to Guatemala from the Inter-American Development Bank to build a rural telecommunications system.

If the administration blinks at human rights abuses in El Salvador and Guatemala, it is more outspoken in criticizing the violations of human rights in Nicaragua than in any other nation in the world. Every real or imagined abuse of human rights by the Sandinist government is proclaimed from the housetops. The rhetoric is grounded more in the administration's opposition to the ideology of the government in Managua than to any concern for human rights. Indeed it seems clear that the activities of the U.S. government in giving support to the anti-Sandinist guerrillas provide a rationale or an excuse for the abuses of human rights engaged in by the Nicaraguan government.

The pattern in Paraguay is similar to that in Central America. The United States, reversing previous policy, voted in favor of a $7.8 million loan from the Inter-American Development Bank to Paraguay. The State Department claimed an improvement in human rights, a claim that cannot be squared with the findings of Amnesty International. The fact is that the state of siege suspending constitutional guarantees continues in effect in Paraguay, as it has since 1954.

The Reagan White House also voted in favor of a $40 million loan to Uruguay despite the fact that Uruguay has one of the highest ratios of political prisoners to population of any country in the world. The pervasive opposition to communism that is so ingrained in President Reagan's approach to Latin America results in support for the Duvalier government in Haiti. Partly because of the opposition of this regime to Castro, the Reagan administration is unwilling to grant political asylum to the several thousand Haitians currently seeking in the United States. But the administration, seeing an apparently communist regime in Ethiopia, decided in July 1982 to provide temporary refuge to some 15,000 Ethiopians in the United States. Minimizing further the extent of human rights violations in Haiti, the administration has authorized the granting of direct foreign assistance to that country as well as credits and guarantees under the Arms Export Control Act.

An attitude that gives priority to encouraging anticommunist regimes over emphasizing human rights is also central to President Reagan's foreign policy outside of Latin America. In South Korea the administration reversed prior U.S. policy of abstaining on loans to that country in various multilateral lending institutions. In 1981 and 1982 the United States voted to support over $300 million in loans to Korea. In September 1982 the Commerce Department cleared the sale of 500 electric shock batons to Korea for "crowd control." The State Department protested and the administration postponed the sale indefinitely.

The administration is claiming that the release of Kim Dae Jung to come to the United States for medical treatment is a triumph for its policy of "quiet diplomacy." There may be some truth in this claim, but the fact remains, as the South Korean opposition leader Mr. Kim noted in Washington on December 24, 1982, that his political followers in Korea do not enjoy freedom to form trade unions or participate in the political process.

Military considerations have also brought about an easing in human rights standards in America's relationship with the Philippines. In 1982 the United States, reversing previous policy, voted in favor of 15 loans totaling over $107 million from the multilateral development banks to the Philippines. The warm reception given by the White House to President Marcos in September 1982 apparently did not result in any agreement by the Marcos government to be more observant of human rights.

A combination of anti-communist and promilitary sentiment has brought about an alteration of America's traditional policies toward South Africa. While condemning apartheid, the Reagan administration has extended financial assistance to the all-white government in Pretoria. The Commerce Department has issued at least 12 licenses for the sale of high technology, and the Reagan administration, on November 3, 1982 supported a loan of over $1 billion from the International Monetary Fund to South Africa. The annual State Department report on the status of human rights required by the Congress last year claimed without supporting evidence that South Africa is moving towards a "modification" of apartheid and that "political change as an organic process is underway in South Africa."

The perception of Zaire as a bulwark against Soviet influence in Africa has led the administration to increase aid to that nation even though the regime of President Mobutu has not been known since it began in 1965 as a regime that respects human rights.

The muting of criticism concerning violations of human rights in nations that are friendly to the United States changes radically in the Reagan administration's approach to communist countries. The imposition of martial law in Poland brought an avalanche of rhetoric and the imposition of economic sanctions against the Soviet Union. After Western Europe defied the prohibition of the transfer of U.S. technology to aid in the construction of the Soviet Union's natural gas pipeline, the Reagan administration was required, in effect, to withdraw the proposal even though the human rights situation in Poland had not improved.

The Reagan administration was also tough on Rumania because of its new heavy education tax on those who desire to emigrate. The administration is similarly aggressive and articulate on abuses of human rights within the Soviet Union. The imprisonment of Helsinki monitors, the continued exile of Andrei Sakharov and the abuse of psychiatry have all been eloquently denounced.

It is uncertain, however, whether this policy is working to help Soviet Jews who desire to emigrate. In 1982 the number permitted to leave the Soviet Union sank to 2,680, the lowest number since 1970 when emigration began. The total for 1982 contrasts sharply with the 9,447 permitted to leave in 1981 and the total of 51,320 granted exit visas in 1979.

The termination of the grain embargo and the offering of a long-term grain deal to the Soviet Union appeared to be contrary to the most fundamental premises of the Reagan administration, especially since not even an attempt was made to obtain human rights concessions in exchange for the sale of grain. One can presumably expect the continuation of the sharp contrast in the different approach to totalitarian and authoritarian nations, even though that vocabulary has now been de-emphasized within administration circles. It is an approach at variance with fundamentals of human rights law as enacted by the Congress starting in 1974. As a result, it has united all of the human rights groups. They were brought together by their successful fight against the proposed appointment of Ernest Lefever as the Assistant Secretary of State for Human Rights.

Since that time human-rights activists have been trying to limit the damage to human rights by the negative policies of the Reagan administration. The task of these groups in the next two years is overwhelming. It is their job to try to blunt the devastating impact on dissidents and insurgents around the world of a policy perceived by them to be one that minimizes, if not eliminates, human rights as a factor in U.S. foreign policy. These people felt that the United States made a significant, even a monumental, contribution to the growth of human freedom by the adoption and the enforcement of a policy which disassociated the United States from violations of those human rights that are internationally recognized as the minimum safeguards for a civilized society. What these people are asking, along with human rights activists everywhere, is that the Reagan administration set aside its double standard and be even-handed in its attention to human rights. This administration has tended to use human rights only as a weapon with which to attack its adversaries.

The legislation enacted by the Congress in the 1970's requiring compliance with human rights in non-communist countries is designed not to contradict but to complement the policy of containment of communism adhered to by the United States for some three decades. The policy of containment is based on respect by the United States for the human rights of persons who live under totalitarian governments. The human rights dimension of U.S. foreign policy that developed in the six years before the Reagan administration was designed to broaden the mandate and the mission of the United States in advancing human rights everywhere in the world. Ultimately that mandate came, of course, from international law and the Charter of the United Nations which in articles 55 and 56 makes the "promotion" of human rights an essential function of the United Nations and an important and inescapable duty of each of its members.

One likes to think that the human rights dimension to U.S. foreign policy has been too institutionalized by Congress and has become too attractive to the entire world for any one administration to be able to eliminate it as an integral and important part of America's foreign policy. But what may remain of that policy after two more years of the Reagan administration is not certain. Clearly the first two years of that administration are not reassuring that the promotion of human rights will be a very important part of U. S. foreign policy in January 1985.

Chapter 4

Argentine Church Should Speak

I shall never be able to forget a day of 14 hours spent in Buenos Aires in November 1976 listening to a description of the disappearances of hundreds of people given by their survivors. I was a member of a team sent by Amnesty International to investigate the terror that descended on Argentina after the military took over that country on March 24, 1976. The delegation from Amnesty International set up a hearing outside a public building, and from 10 a.m. to midnight we heard hundreds of wives and parents relate the circumstances under which their husbands or children disappeared.

What will the new civilian government that took over Argentina December 10, 1983, do about an accounting of the "disappeared," estimated to be between 6,000 and 30,000? One likes to think that the eight-year nightmare of military rule is done and that peace of some kind can come to the Argentines. But the new president, Raul Alfonsin, a 56-year-old country lawyer, will aggravate the military if he pushes too far to bring to trial the members of the death squads who committed mass murder.

At the same time, Alfonsin must be faithful to his promise in the campaign that "he will insist on cleaning up" the cases of those who disappeared under military rule. But Alfonsin had not been very specific as to what he could or might do to vindicate the rights of the victims and their survivors.

No one knows exactly what might happen in Argentina.

First published in the *National Catholic Reporter*, December 30, 1983.

Since 1930, Argentina has been ruled by seven civilian presidents and 15 military presidents. None of the seven civilians finished his six-year term.

I have been thinking of the families I met and whose tragedy struck me in 1976. I have been in touch with some of them. It is impossible to understand the depths of their suffering. A distinguished man, Emilio Mignone, whose daughter Monica had recently disappeared, was one of the first persons I met in Buenos Aires in 1976. A lawyer and a former president of a university, Mignone had access to the highest levels of government but he could discover nothing about the four plainclothesmen who came early one morning to take Monica away. She was never seen again. No charge had ever been brought against her nor was she political in any way. She was a teacher of poor children.

Mignone is now the head of the Center for Legal and Social Studies. This unit has been collecting all available information on the disappeared since this gruesome phenomenon became a feature of life in Argentina. Mignone will be in the eye of the storm as the world watches to see if the Alfonsin government can correct a 400 per cent annual inflation, manage a $40 billion foreign debt, decrease a 12 per cent unemployment rate and bring about reconciliation in a nation torn apart by government-sponsored mass murders that touched almost everyone.

The outgoing military government sought to insulate itself from liability for the disappeared. In August it announced an amnesty for everyone in government who committed any crimes intended to end subversion. The federal courts in Argentina may not accept this blanket self-amnesty. The Catholic bishops, moreover, may articulate their opposition to it because for several months they have been demanding an accounting from the government and have called such an accounting essential to national reconciliation.

An accounting for the dead and disappeared may theoretically be possible because the military in Argentina are now in disgrace. They managed the war in the Falklands as badly as they managed the economy. The military demonstrated such incapacity to manage anything that presumably the people of

Argentina will not want them returned to power.

But the military has always had a powerful hold on the minds of the Argentines. They might exploit that power by claiming Alfonsin is "soft" on communism because he believes in human rights. During the eight years of Argentina's dark night of the soul, Alfonsin was active in the small human rights movement in his country and has openly proclaimed that thousands in Argentina were saved because of the human rights policies of the U.S. Congress and the Carter administration.

The hierarchy of Argentina has not generally been outspoken and forceful like the bishops of Chile or Brazil. The bishops of Argentina have sometimes been thought of as the most conservative in Latin America. With the return of democracy to Argentina, they have an opportunity to add the influence of the Catholic church to the voice of the "mothers of the Plaza de Mayo" whose Thursday demonstrations in behalf of the disappeared have been one of the major reasons for the restoration of democracy in Argentina.

In late 1976, many Catholic leaders in Argentina appeared to acquiesce in what the government at that time was going in the name of eliminating communists in what was called a "dirty war." Since that time, Catholic leaders have become much more militant. They now have a unique and supreme opportunity to insert the principles of Medellin and Puebla into the political and legal life of Argentina.

PART II

World Hunger

Chapter 5

The World Food Situation

Mr. Speaker, it is generally conceded that the current world food situation has reached crisis proportions and that we are at a crossroads in determining the fact of life or death for untold millions of human beings, now and in the years to come.

According to the United Nations Food and Agricultural Organization, at least 15,000 people die of malnutrition daily. Ten thousand of them are children. At least 460 million people are severely affected by malnutrition around the world. Ninety-four percent of those so affected, according to the "Assessment of the World Food Situation" prepared for the World Food Conference, live in developing countries.

The United States has had a longstanding policy of helping the developing nations help themselves. House Concurrent Resolution 393, introduced in the House by my distinguished colleague from Minnesota (Mr. Fraser), would explicitly express our national policy as being one which recognizes the right to food and thus continue our humanitarian traditions. House Concurrent Resolution 393, of which I am proud to be a cosponsor, recognizes the responsibility of the United States at this time of growing food shortages.

What are some of the factors which have contributed to this global insecurity on the food supply front? Briefly, this stage was set by the convergence of the following circumstances:

A dangerous drop in food reserves. During the period since World War II there have been two major safety valves: cropland held idle in the United States under Government subsidy

First published in the *Congressional Record*, January 8, 1976.

programs, and carryover stocks of grain in the principal export-
ing countries. The United States has brought all of the previously idle cropland — 50 million acres — into production,
beginning with the food crisis years of 1966 and 1967 and
culminating with almost full production in 1974 in response to
the ever worsening food situation. Simultaneously, global food
reserves were dangerously depleted.

Energy shortage and increased energy costs. This situation, a
result of the natural law of diminishing natural fuels as well as
governmental decisions regarding pricing and distribution of
these fuels, has had and will continue to have disastrous effects
on the global hunger problem. In developing countries, the
rising prices of oil imports will tend to absorb the money
needed for the importation of fertilizer, which has also risen in
price. Energy is also essential for the production of fertilizer,
and a reduced amount of fertilizer has a direct effect on food
supply. It is estimated that 1 million tons of fertilizer are
required to turn out 9 or 10 million tons of grain. Energy is also
crucial for other processes associated with food production,
such as irrigation and transportation.

Increased population. The impact of world population
growth on food demand is obvious. The current unprecedented
rate of world population growth is 2 percent annually, which
brings a doubling — of both people and of demand for food —
every 35 years.

Increased demand for protein. This demand is a result not
only of increased population, but of growing affluence
throughout the world. It may seem curious that a rising per
capita income can contribute to the world food problem, bound
as it is with increased agricultural production, improved standards of living, and lowered death rates, all highly desirable
from many points of view. However, higher per capita income
can escalate demand for food just as surely and inexorably as
increased population. For instance, during the drought in 1972,
the Russians chose not to slaughter cattle as they had in previous
droughts, but rather to import grain in order to maintain a
higher standard of living. This in turn depleted U.S. grain
reserves and created a sharp rise in grain prices throughout the
world.

Although the world hunger outlook is frightening, it is not hopeless. There are many areas in which substantial progress can be made, assuming that the desire for positive change and the information for intelligent choices are available.

The chain of events triggered by the Russian decision to buy grain rather than slaughter cattle illustrates the interdependency of countries. The hunger crisis must be approached as a global problem rather than simply a national one. Research efforts and policies affecting the food situation must be coordinated and studied harmoniously. In an attempt to meet this objective, the World Food Council of the United Nations, meeting for the first time in June 1975, simply stated its task: "to supervise and improve the way men grow their food and the way they share it among themselves."

Lower rates of population growth are also a feasible and reasonable objective. Many developing countries experienced significant decreases in birth rates in the 1960's. Although the problem is not merely one of restricting births — experience having shown that birthrates do not decline sharply unless basic social needs are met — a well-organized and socially responsible program to furnish information in this area is essential.

There is also room for hope in the area of increasing farm yields, surely the key to feeding a hungry world. A National Research Council study on world food and nutrition estimated that between 1948 and 1971 "each dollar of science-oriented research generated an annual benefit of about $31 in developed countries and $80 in developing countries." As the report states, these figures are significant proof of the returns feasible from food production research. The figures also indicate that these benefits are much larger when there is international linking of research activities.

All of these improvements in the world hunger picture require a reordering of national global priorities, a reexamination of just what constitutes a threat to human security and well-being. Rapidly accumulating evidence suggests that threats to humanity today are not so much the traditional ones of conflict and invasion by foreign powers, but a result of ecological stresses. Governments will continue to pour money into armaments rather than food production research, however, until they can be convinced of a need to do otherwise.

It is finally the private citizen who has the responsibility to convince the leadership that the time for change has come. And, indeed, there are indications that the American people are mobilizing on behalf of the less fortunate throughout the world. Various private organizations are disseminating valuable information to all interested persons as to how best to influence public policy for the good of the hungry. Bread for the World is one such organization with excellent sources of information, a dedicated leadership, and a growing membership. With available resources such as these the private citizen in the United States has the opportunity to directly challenge elected officials to fulfill the promise of our humanitarian traditions and seek to avert hunger for future generations around the world.

Chapter 6

The Right to Food

Mr. Speaker, I am pleased to rise in support of House Concurrent Resolution 737, the right-to-food resolution. This resolution constitutes a reaffirmation and strengthening of the principles accepted by the United States and other participating nations at the World Food Conference in Rome in 1974. At that time, the United States proposed and the conference adopted a fundamental objective stating that:

> Within a decade no child will go to bed hungry, that no family will fear for its next day's bread, and that no human being's future and capacities will be stunted by malnutrition.

One-fifth of that decade has now passed, Mr. Speaker, but we are no closer to fulfilling that historic pledge. World food aid did increase during 1975-76 to 9 million tons, but that amount was still 1 million tons shy of the goal set a year earlier. Even more significantly, only half of the 1 million tons of fertilizer aid targeted for developing nations was actually contributed in the past year. Harvests were generally excellent throughout the world in both 1975 and 1976, yet world food stocks increased only slightly over their dangerously depleted levels of 1974. World fertilizer production continues to lag behind demand.

Meanwhile, the population of the developing nations continues to rise at a rapid rate. Each day the need for adequate nourishment grows more acute. Each day, thousands of human beings die of starvation and diseases brought on by malnutri-

First published in the *Congressional Record*, September 21, 1976.

tion. Many climatologists and meterologists are predicting that the world is entering a period to be characterized by severe local droughts and overall poor growing conditions. All of these alarming facts make prompt and effective action essential if we are to stave off massive worldwide famine in the years ahead.

The right-to-food resolution, which I have co-sponsored, does not in itself provide the solution to that enormous and critical problem. As I noted in testifying before the International Relations Subcommittee on International Resources, Food, and Energy on June 24th, "the right-to-food resolution is merely an expression of opinion by the Congress; its enactment will not in itself prevent a single person from starving." Yet, as an indication of our determination and commitment to control this universal problem, House Concurrent Resolution 737 is an important first step.

With the passage of this resolution here today, we will join the Senate in demonstrating to the developing nations throughout the world that the United States is not going to abandon them as they seek a means of feeding their people. As the resolution states, we must increase our level of food assistance to the most seriously affected countries. We must also accelerate our efforts to join with other food exporters in establishing an international food reserve. Our scientists and engineers must expand their research to discover better fertilizers and more efficient forms of land management to help increase worldwide food production. We should also continue to provide our technological and practical expertise to developing nations seeking to improve family planning among their people. The passage of the right-to-food resolution does none of these things, but it creates an impetus for all of them.

Mr. Speaker, I am pleased to note that both the House and Senate committees which considered this resolution credit the organization, Bread for the World, with formulating the right-to-food concept and actively promoting its adoption by the Congress. Bread for the World is an interdenominational Christian citizens movement working to alleviate world hunger. I am privileged to serve as a member of the board of directors of Bread for the World.

Chapter 7

Health Care: A Dream Deferred

In 1982, 40,000 children died every day. Fourteen million died during the 12 months. Most of these deaths were caused by malnutrition and infection. Almost all of them were preventable.

That is the grim message of the 36th annual report of UNICEF (United Nations Children's Fund). But that sad message is mingled with a clear and convincing prediction by UNICEF that the adoptions of four low-cost remedies would within a decade cut in half the daily deaths of children. They are programs for oral rehydration therapy, universal child immunization, the promotion of breast-feeding and the mass use of child-growth charts. These proposals merit attention.

1. Dehydration caused by diarrheal infection now kills an estimated five million young children each year. It is by far the largest single cause of death for children in the developing world. The average child will have this infection between six and 16 times per year. Until recently severe dehydration could be corrected only by expensive intravenous feeding in an often inaccessible hospital. Now it has been discovered that a solution of glucose and salt can markedly increase the body's rate of absorption of fluid. The *Lancet*, a prestigious British medical journal, has written that this discovery is potentially "the most important medical advance this century."

UNICEF is making oral rehydration packets available in Nicaragua, Haiti, Bangladesh and elsewhere. These programs

First published in the *National Catholic Reporter*, February 18, 1983.

31

are very effective, but the struggle has just begun to stop a child from dying every six seconds from dehydration.

2. Six diseases kill five million children every year — measles, diphtheria, tetanus, whooping cough, poliomyelitis and tuberculosis. Tetanus alone kills a million youngsters a year, measles claims 1.5 million victims.

The cost of immunizing a child from these diseases has decreased substantially. Measles vaccine now costs less than 10 cents per dose. Many vaccines now no longer require refrigeration. The World Health Organization has long worked to make it feasible for all of the earth's children to receive those immunizations (and repeated booster shots where necessary), which children in developed nations receive routinely.

3. As the percentage of babies being breast-fed increases, the number of malnourished infants declines. The UNICEF report flatly predicts that if the campaign to foster breast-feeding were intensive enough, one million infant lives a year could be saved within a decade.

4. If mothers were taught what weight and size to expect of their children, they would be alerted to the malnutrition which is very often invisible. To accomplish this object, UNICEF recommends the mass use of simple child-growth charts. These charts are used by two million mothers in 15,000 villages in Indonesia with salutary results.

These four opportunities, the UNICEF report notes, are "all low-cost, low-risk, low-resistance." They are also "available now." They constitute paradoxically a way by which the developing countries can slow down their rates of population growth. This is true because, as the report states, "when people become more confident that their existing children will survive, they tend to have fewer births." This is such a predictable phenomenon that the UNICEF report affirms that it is the "principal reason why no nation has ever seen a significant and sustained fall in its birthrate without first seeing a fall in its child death rate."

The UNICEF report documents the fact that the fall in the death rate of children was accompanied by an even larger fall in the birthrate in nations like Thailand, Costa Rica and the Philippines. Consequently, UNICEF predicts that if the infant and child mortality rate of the Third World was halved by the year 2000, there would be up to 20 million fewer births each year!

A national commitment is needed, writes James P. Grant, the executive director of UNICEF. If that commitment is not given or renewed, "the number of children who will die each year will be the equivalent of the entire under-five population of the United States!"

The Congress heard the cries of protest against the attempt of the Reagan administration to cut the U.S. appropriation to UNICEF. As I noted in these pages (*NCR*, April 9, 1982), the White House proposed a slash in the U.S. payment to UNICEF from $41.5 million to $26.6 million. In December 1982, the Congress appropriated $42.5 million for UNICEF for 1983. That result came about because members of Bread for the World and similar groups intensively lobbied the Congress. One senator, for example, received over 1,000 communications urging an increase in the allotment to UNICEF.

The Congress, at least for now, shares the hope set forth in this concluding sentence of the UNICEF report:

> If the political will can be found to seize the opportunities now offered by recent social and scientific progress, then the goal of adequate food and health for the vast majority of the world's children need not be a dream deferred.

Chapter 8

Narcissistic America Ignores World Hunger

The presence and extent of hunger among Americans is a subject that will not go away in 1984. But it is a sign of the narcissism of the American people that there are very few voices of concern raised about hunger across the world.

Global hunger and malnutrition go on in the global village. Two billion people live on incomes below $500 a year. At least one person in five is trapped in absolute poverty. In the Third World, one in three who wants to work cannot find a regular job; there are 600 million people who have no job or who are less than fully employed.

About half of humanity do not have a dependable supply of safe water to drink. At least 450 million people suffer from chronic hunger and malnutrition.

The number of illiterates continues to rise. Illiteracy among women is rising faster than among men. By an estimate in a volume edited by Ruth Leger Sivard, titled *World Military and Social Expenditures 1983*, in 1990 there will be 539 million illiterate women and 345 million men who cannot read or write. There are now 120 million children (one-third of all of those between the ages of six and 11) who are not in school.

Eleven million of those to be born in 1984 will die before their fifth birthday. As of 1980, less than 10 per cent of children in the Third World were being immunized against the common

First published in the *National Catholic Reporter*, January 20, 1984.

diseases of childhood. To give these immunizations would cost $5 a child.

All of this is made much more bleak by the fact that by the year 2000 the global population will expand by at least 1.7 billion people. This will bring the present total of 4.2 billion inhabitants to almost 6 billion. Little if anything is being done to prepare for the 1.7 billion new human beings who will be in the world 16 years from now. Eighty-five per cent of them will reside in underdeveloped countries.

If the land now being cultivated in the Third World is to meet the growing demands for food, each arable acre will have to feed twice as many people as it did in 1975.

U.S. foreign policy is almost oblivious to these problems. This year the federal government is paying farmers to take nearly 100 million acres of cropland out of production.

The problem of hunger in the underdeveloped nations is further complicated by the new and frightening phenomenon of the debts of these countries. Their total debt, $90 billion in 1971, rose by 1982 to a staggering $626 billion. Even the interest charges on these loans can cripple the economies of these debtor nations.

A further reason for the widespread malnutrition of almost one-half billion people is the unbelievable expenditure of underdeveloped nations for arms. The global sum for arms has now reached $660 billion a year. In many nations, the government spends far more on armaments than on health and education combined.

It is true, of course, that immense progress has been made in improving the nutritional levels of developing nations. At a conference I attended in the recent past on food for the world, the morale of the experts was upbeat and optimistic. But even these professionals on the problems of the Third World still warned that the future is unpredictable and grim.

Is there not something inappropriate about having a national debate — or at least a national shouting match — about the extent of hunger in America and never once mentioning the misery of hunger beyond our borders? At least in America the food exists, and the problem could be abated if the food could be distributed more competently. But in parts of Africa and

Asia, the food that is urgently needed simply does not exist.

Everyone should be reminded that for the first time in 16 years poor people are increasing in America. They now number 34 million, 15 per cent of the population. But everyone should also remember that if Americans forget the hungry of the world they hurt themselves and do an injustice to millions of people now and in the years to come. The safety, and even the survival, of these people depends on the foreign policy of the U.S. government. In 1974, at the world meeting of the Food and Agriculture Organization (FAO) in Rome, the United States made a pledge that within a decade no child in the world would go to bed hungry. That promise has not been fulfilled.

Chapter 9

House Hunger Commission Urged

The tragedy and horror of millions of starving people keep coming back to me. I recall vividly the Rome forum in November 1974, called by the late Barbara Ward to give recommendations to the forthcoming World Food Conference. I recall even more vividly these words of then Secretary of State Henry Kissinger in his address, opening the conference:

> The profound promise of our era is that for the first time we have the technical capacity to free mankind from the scourge of hunger. Therefore, today we must proclaim a bold objective that within a decade no child will go to bed hungry.

President Gerald Ford's administration appeared to be committed and courageous at that Rome conference a decade ago. But, alas, the number of children going to bed hungry has not diminished. In June 1983 the World Food Council reported that "450 million are chronomically underfed, while 40 million die from malnutrition every year, about four million of them children."

Why has the commitment of the United States government been so unsteady and unreliable? How can an administration almost obsessed with the question of furnishing surgery to Baby Jane Doe be so little concerned that, as the United Nations Children's Fund (UNICEF) reported recently, five million

First published in the *National Catholic Reporter*, March 23, 1984.

children died last year from dehydration caused by diarrhea, three million more from pneumonia and two million from measles?

A 1983 UNICEF report stated that recently available methods could save half the 40,000 children in the world who die every day. A relatively modest increase in UNICEF's $350 million annual budget would allow this organization, which operates in 115 countries, to save 20,000 lives a day.

Why doesn't the United States try to furnish that amount or help to raise it among our allies? The Kissinger report on Central America, by urging the expenditure of about $8 billion for five years for assistance to Central America, recognized that economic insecurity breeds political instability that can be a threat to America's national security. Is there any logical reason that this concept should not apply to most nations in the world?

American aid to the Third World continues to decline. In the past seven years, U.S. aid as a percentage of its gross national product, declined more than in any Western industrial country. Indeed, in recent years, the United States gave proportionately less of its wealth to poor countries than almost any other non-communist nation gave.

The Organization for Economic Cooperation and Development (OECD), in its recent annual report, noted that the United States gave only .23 per cent of its gross national product to foreign aid — the lowest of any of the 24 OECD nations except Italy.

The United States is a long way from the .7 per cent of gross national product for foreign aid recommended by the United Nations. The Netherlands, Sweden, Norway and Denmark are the only Western nations to meet the UN target.

Another recent decision of the Reagan administration affects the Third World adversely. After years during which the United States provided up to 40 per cent of all the funds for the International Development Fund, the subsidizing arm of the World Bank, the White House imposed a ceiling of $750 million and restricted aid to 25 per cent of the budget of this international agency in 1984 through 1986. This is hardly a generous gesture for a nation that has more than one-third of the entire gross national product of the world.

Another indication of the reluctance of the Reagan administration to alleviate world hunger is the controversy within the administration about continued U.S. financing of the International Fund for Agricultural Development (IFAD), an agency that grew out of the 1974 World Food Conference in Rome.

The IFAD has a $1.8 billion budget and gets its funding almost equally from the industrialized nations and the Organization of Petroleum Exporting Countries (OPEC). It has extended millions of loans to farmers in 77 countries. The United States is in arrears on its full financial pledge to the agency. The future role of U.S. participation will be high on the agenda when the IFAD meets in Rome February 29 to consider a new series of multi-year financial pledges.

In a recent fund-raising letter, the chairman of the U.S. Committee for UNICEF, Hugh Downs, wrote these moving words:

> In the 10 seconds it took you to open and begin this letter, three children died from the effects of malnutrition somewhere in the world.
>
> No statistic can express what it's like to see even one child die that way...to see a mother sitting hour after hour, leaning her child's body against her own...to watch the small feeble head movements that expend all the energy a youngster has left...to see the panic in a dying tot's innocent eyes...and then to know in a moment that life is gone.

How can the U.S. government fail to respond to such an appeal? Has Congress forgotten the urgent recommendations of President Jimmy Carter's commission on World Hunger? Don't the White House and Congress have some sense of decency about trying to fulfill Kissinger's commitment made on behalf of the nation in 1974?

In the near future, the U.S. House of Representatives will vote on the establishment of a House select committee on hunger, HR 15. This measure was reported favorably November 17, 1983, by the House Rules Committee. The focus of that proposed unit is more on domestic hunger rather than on global starvation. But if a select committee on hunger becomes a reality, it may be one more way to remind the United States government that it has promises to keep.

PART III

Arms Control

Chapter 10

U.S. Arms Sales a Growing Threat to Peace

Mr. Speaker, after a record $8.3 billion in orders for foreign military sales in fiscal 1974, the export of American weapons is increasing still further in the current year. The United States contributes more to foreign arsenals through arms sales than the rest of the world combined. In 1974, American arms were sold to 70 foreign governments including a large number of repressive military dictatorships in Latin America, Africa, and Asia. In these countries, our arms help to perpetuate the subjugation of the people of the existing government.

The most dangerous facet of our foreign military sales program is our role in the Middle East, which has purchased the preponderance of American arms exports during the past few years. While the administration purports to be working for a peaceful settlement of the Middle East conflict and to reduce the risk of renewed hostilities, it has supplied vast quantities of arms to Iran, Saudi Arabia, Jordan, and other nations in this volatile part of the world. By expanding the arsenals of virtually all parties in the Middle East and Persian Gulf regions, the United States has made it easier for war to be waged and helped to insure that any future war will be more tragic and destructive than the last. The enormous expansion of arms sales to Middle Eastern nations has been carried out by the administration without the prior knowledge or consent of Congress. I have introduced H.R. 4133 in the House, similar to legislation

First published in the *Congressional Record*, April 16, 1975.

filed in the Senate by Senator Kennedy, which would suspend the sale of arms to Persian Gulf nations for 6 months unless Congress approves a comprehensive policy statement on such sales submitted by the president.

It is imperative that Congress participate in all decisions to sell weapons to various countries throughout the world. Until this year, Congress' only involvement in this key aspect of our foreign policy was in receiving periodic reports after the fact on sales completed in the recent past. At that point, it was, of course, too late for Congress to act against any sale it did not approve of. An amendment to the Foreign Military Sales Act, contained within the Foreign Assistance Act of 1974, constituted the first significant step toward meaningful congressional oversight of proposed arms sales. That amendment provides for prior congressional notification of all proposed sales valued above $25 million carried out under the Foreign Military Sales Act. Congress then has 20 days in which to disapprove a proposed sale by concurrent resolution.

These recently enacted oversight requirements have a number of major loopholes which must be closed through appropriate legislation. First, the amendment adopted in 1974 applies only to sales conducted under the Foreign Military Sales Act. The export of weapons by private corporations and nongovernmental agencies is regulated under the provisions of the Mutual Security Act, which grants sole regulatory power to the president. On February 19, 1975, I introduced H.R. 3213 which would subject all proposed arms exports under the Mutual Security Act to the provisions of prior congressional notification and congressional disapproval contained in the Foreign Assistance Act of 1974. I am pleased to report that 45 of my colleagues have joined me in sponsoring this bill to date.

A second deficiency of existing provisions for congressional oversight in the field of foreign arms sales is the exemption of all sales valued at less than $25 million. From the standpoint of American foreign policy, it is the destination of the arms, rather than their cash value, which is of greatest significance. A relatively small sale of arms to South Africa or Hungary, for example, would have enormous implications for the conduct of our foreign policy. It is therefore necessary that Congress have prior notice and veto power over all proposed foreign weapons sales, regardless of the size of a transaction.

On April 7, 1975, I introduced H.R. 5659 which eliminates the exemption from oversight of all proposed arms sales valued at less than $25 million. The bill also establishes special procedures for the consideration of resolutions disapproving particular proposed arms sales to insure that Congress has an opportunity to complete action on such resolutions within the 20-day oversight period specified by law. I plan to circulate a Dear Colleague letter later this week to ask for the support of my colleagues on this piece of legislation.

No amount of congressional oversight conducted on a piecemeal basis, however, can effectively replace a set of consistent policies governing the sale of arms to foreign countries which will best serve the foreign policy objectives of the United States and the overall interests of world peace. This type of leadership has been sadly lacking as the administration has greatly expanded authorized arms sales during the past few years. An intensive evaluation of the possible consequences of massive arms sales by the United States to nations throughout the world is long overdue. Congress should seriously consider placing strict limits on additional arms sales until such an evaluation has been completed and fully considered by Congress.

Are Arms a Way Out of War?

In mid-December in Washington at the annual meeting of the Arms Control Association, the nation's most knowledgeable and experienced arms controllers candidly confessed their deep apprehension over what the Reagan administration might do about the Strategic Arms Limitation Talks (SALT II).

The meeting, held at the elegant offices of the Carnegie Endowment for Peace on the day before the announcement of Alexander Haig as secretary of state, centered on the desirability of recreating that consensus on arms control which existed in public opinion and possibly in the Senate before the invasion of Afghanistan. SALT II, which once had three-to-one support among the public, may now once again be postponed indefinitely.

The opponents of SALT II seem to have out-organized its friends. But if no revision of SALT II is advanced by the Reagan administration during the next four years, will the Soviets, bound by no limitations, increase their weapons and attain superiority? And if so, will this alarming result be charged to the Reagan administration?

Assuming that the answer to both of those questions is yes, how can the advocates of arms control develop a public consensus demanding prompt action to ratify some form of SALT II?

No one associated with arms control thinks that it will be easy to reawaken public opinion favorable to arms reduction.

First published in the *National Catholic Reporter*, January 23, 1981.

The topic is too arcane for easy comprehension or familiar conversation; terms like Poseidon, Trident, backfire bombers and SS-18s leave almost everyone baffled. Furthermore, the administration might embrace superiority rather than sufficiency and thereby cloud over the necessity of SALT II.

In addition, the Reagan administration might curtail the $17.5 million budget for the Arms Control and Disarmament Agency (ACDA) and thus mute the one federal agency charged by Congress with the task of proposing methods to reduce arms. The new administration, moreover, might openly embrace "linkage" and thereby condition any further negotiations on SALT II on better behavior by the Soviets.

Even more distressing is the possibility of tinkering with the ABM treaty — the only major strategic arms control agreement in existence, and the prize of SALT I.

In the background of all discussions of strategic weapons is the absence of any clear U.S. policy integrating nuclear and conventional warfare. There are suggestions from some that a nuclear war is "winnable." Others feel that President Carter was unrealistic when he pledged in his first inaugural address to work for the total elimination of all nuclear weapons.

The 1980 meeting of the Arms Control Association was admittedly one of the gloomiest in the history of that group. Those assembled were reminded by Gerald Smith, U.S. negotiator for SALT and former director of ACDA, that the United States and the USSR "which between them can destroy civilization...are bound to struggle to find a way out." That way will "only open up if it is to their common advantage," he said.

Solemn words indeed as the United States enters a presidency which will last through 1984!

Chapter 12

No Soviet Winning Streak

Behind the policy the administration is following with regard to El Salvador appears to be the hidden assumption that Moscow is having a "winning streak." The State Department and the Pentagon want to show the Kremlin and the world the U.S. can stop Soviet momentum.

The reality is, however, that the Soviets have been unable to command loyalty or obedience in most nations where they have infiltrated. Russia's enormous setbacks during the past several years dwarf any marginal Soviet advances in certain countries.

The facts do *not* support any perceptions of consistent Soviet advances and devastating U.S. setbacks.

Under any interpretation of world history during the past 35 years, there is no evidence to suggest there has been a sustained, persistent Soviet geopolitical momentum.

The high point of the Kremlin's influence was in 1958, when Russian influence in China and in Indonesia was significant. The Sino-Soviet split in 1960, with the spectacular defection of mainland China, brought about that the USSR and Peking are now bitter enemies with apparently no chance for rapprochement.

In 1965, another major blow came to the Kremlin when Indonesia dissolved its relationship with the Soviet Union, with General Suharto breaking all ties with Russia. The USSR had poured billions of dollars into this nation in the years 1958-1965, only to see Indonesia become vehemently anti-Communist.

First published in the *National Catholic Reporter*, April 24, 1981.

For 25 years, the Soviets poured billions into the Middle East; the only nation that still supports Russia in that part of the world is tiny, destitute South Yemen.

The same situation has developed with respect to Egypt, which received $2.7 billion from Russia, but in 1972, repudiated its $5 billion debt to the USSR and expelled 20,000 Soviet technicians.

Some 10 African nations during the past 35 years have had some significant Soviet influence, but now, Russia influences only four — Angola, Mozambique, Ethiopia and Algeria — of 50 nations.

In Asia, the story is similar. The Soviet Union gave $5 billion to India, and during the years 1962-1977, India was virtually an ally of the Soviet Union. That special relationship ended abruptly in 1977, when Morarji Desai defeated Indira Gandhi for the prime ministry. India, one of the founders of the non-aligned movement, has denied military basing privileges to the Soviets and openly opposes a permanent Soviet presence in the Indian Ocean.

In Vietnam, there is, at least temporarily, some Soviet influence. Five thousand Soviet technicians are in Vietnam, with perhaps $800 million per year going to that country to carry out its illegal invasion of neutral Cambodia. But one can be certain that Vietnam, after struggling for 1,000 years to expel the Chinese, after having fought for almost a century to win its independence from France, and after struggling for more years to defeat the United States, is not about to become a client state or a satellite of the Kremlin.

In all of Latin America, the USSR has only one nation under its control — Cuba. Even in Afghanistan, which the Soviets invaded, resistance is vigorous to the attempt to Sovietize this backward country. The people of Afghanistan, furthermore, are fiercely independent; they have been fighting off outsiders since Alexander the Great, Genghis Khan and the Mongol and British empires.

Fifteen countries in the world at one time were members of the Soviet power system but have broken away from it. The most significant of these nations are China, India, Indonesia, Egypt and Yugoslavia. Other nations which have left the Soviet sphere are Albania, Algeria, Bangladesh, Ghana, Guinea, Iraq, Mali, Somalia, Sudan and North Yemen.

Moscow today controls about six per cent of the population of the world, and about 5.5 per cent of the gross national product (apart from the USSR). But that figure has not changed since the 1950s and early 1960s, when there were major defections from the hegemony of the Soviet Union.

It is disconcerting to see today rhetoric coming from the State Department and the administration which is reminiscent of the cold war statements of the 1950s and early 1960s. It sometimes seems as if détente was never created and never existed.

Détente was both the cause and effect of the Helsinki accords signed in 1975 by 35 European nations, the United States and Canada. Détente can hardly seem to be a living reality when the president of the United States accuses the Soviets of consistently lying and cheating. Such unfortunate rhetoric make negotiations and diplomacy infinitely more difficult.

The invasion of Afghanistan, however inexcusable and reprehensible, does not warrant a total scrapping of détente. The whole world community in the UN General Assembly properly condemned Russia's brutal expropriation of Afghanistan, but the military action in Afghanistan does not justify the United States leaping to the conclusion that the Soviet Union will invade everywhere. Even if that assumption is made, one must note that the Soviet Union is not permitted to remain in the vast majority of countries where it has obtained influence by some wrongful methods.

The trend of Soviet influence has not been increasing; it has been static or even declining. Third World nations do not find a Soviet presence or a Moscow influence attractive. They will permit such influence only if it serves their economic purposes.

Chapter 13

No Nuclear War is Winnable

It is difficult to arouse the emotions of anyone about nuclear weapons now that they have been in the possession of mankind for some 35 years. It is well known that 50,000 nuclear weapons exist, 30,000 of which are in the possession of the United States. It is self-evident that one of these nuclear devices could be detonated by malice, madness or mistake.

One of the more recent reasons for deep concern about nuclear weaponry is the statements made by Vice President George Bush to the effect that a nuclear war is "winnable." The clear assumption for more than 30 years had been that any nuclear war is unthinkable because it is simply not winnable.

Another warning signal came in Presidential Directive 59 issued by President Carter. Although the thrust of this presidential mandate is not entirely clear it seems that Presidential Directive 59 seeks to expand the range of targets beyond the urban-industrial community that has been at the heart of strategic planning for two decades. Presidential Directive 59 appears to be a refinement or modification of a previous policy of "mutually assured destruction" (or MAD). Whatever Presidential Directive 59 may ultimately be or become it clearly is an acknowledgement that the United States is prepared to engage in repeated and limited nuclear exchanges with the Soviet Union.

A third reason for deep concern is the fact that the Pentagon announced in December 1980 that 27 nuclear bomb accidents

First published in the *New Catholic World*, May-June, 1981.

had occurred. The figure may be higher according to the Washington based Center for Defense Information, a private military research group under the direction of retired Admiral Gene LaRocque. This group claims that 95 nuclear accidents occurred between the years 1950 and 1975. The most visible accident occurred in September, 1980 in Arkansas where a Titan II missile exploded killing one Air Force maintenance man and seriously injuring a number of others.

A fourth reason for concern by Catholics and others about the future of U.S. nuclear arms policy comes about from the recent publication of a 150-page book entitled *In Defense of Life*, issued by the military vicariate of the United States. This document seems to claim that the traditional just war doctrine of the Catholic church is not obsolete and that therefore presumably some use of nuclear weapons might be justified.

A fifth reason for concern derives from the proposed use of the neutron bomb. Those who propose the use of this device assert that it would deter the other side with the result that conventional war would be less likely.

Those who are disturbed at these developments can take comfort in the fact that recent moral theology developed in the Second Vatican Council appears to be relatively clear in stating that nuclear weapons may never be used in war either for offensive or defensive purposes. Pope John XXIII in his encyclical *Pacem in Terris* delivered on Easter Sunday, 1963 openly stated that "nuclear weapons should be banned . . . It is hardly possible to imagine that in the atomic era war could be used as an instrument of peace." This document, the last encyclical of Pope John, was extraordinary in every way including the way in which it was received with jubilation by the entire world. Pope John pleaded for mediation and not for militancy, for world peace and not for a world campaign against communism. Rereading *Pacem in Terris* one is reminded of the statement of Gandhi when he said that "human nature is one and therefore unfailingly responds to the advances of love." The world responded to Pope John with prompt and enthusiastic comments from President John Kennedy, Nikita Khruschev and U Thant.

The idealism of *Pacem in Terris* was reflected in the fact that

Pope John expressed great admiration and hope for the United Nations and particularly for the impact of the United Nations Declaration on Human Rights adopted by virtually all the nations of the Earth on December 10, 1948.

Unfortunately the 2,200 Catholic bishops who met in the Second Vatican Council in the years 1962-1965 do not seem to have picked up on the basic thrust of *Pacem in Terris* which is that "nuclear weapons should be banned.... " The Second Vatican Council did, however, assert that it is necessary to undertake an evaluation of war with an "entirely new attitude." Vatican II, pursuant to this principle, sets forth two moral principles as absolutes. The first of these principles is the forbidding as "most infamous" those actions "designed for the methodical extermination of an entire people, nation or ethnic minority." The second principle condemns as a "crime against God and man himself . . . any act of war aimed indiscriminately at the destruction of entire cities or extensive areas along with their population."

It seems rather clear that the Council fathers intended in these two condemnations to condemn nuclear war since, unlike conventional war, nuclear war is by its very nature intended to bring about "the destruction of entire cities or extensive areas along with their population."

The question left unanswered, however, was this: how can the possession of intercontinental ballistic missiles, designed precisely to achieve morally forbidden objectives, be deemed a moral act?

This question was raised by the late Cardinal Joseph Ritter during the fourth session of Vatican II. In his intervention, which was seen only by the members of a conciliar subcommission, Cardinal Ritter asked that the very possession of the arms required for a total war be categorically condemned. The statement of Cardinal Ritter, published shortly after his death, deserves attention. The Cardinal asked this question:

> The possession of those arms which actually constitute the 'balance of terror' even those which are aimed exclusively at deterring an adversary, already involve the intention — conditional perhaps but effective — of using those arms: for

possession without any intention of use would deter no one, would affect nothing. From the very nature of these arms, their enormous quantity and distribution, it can be seen what kind and how great a destruction is already projected. How then are we able to condemn every intention of destroying cities and at the same time, at least in part, approve the balance of terror?

Cardinal Ritter's conclusion in the same document is this:

I believe, therefore, that there should be an absolute condemnation of the possession of arms which involve the intention of the grave peril of total war.

It follows from this, Cardinal Ritter argues, that "there should be a clear and distinct declaration that the moral law requires that all urgently and without delay collaborate in the elimination of the possession of such armaments, no matter how great the difficulties which are feared and must be overcome."

Cardinal Ritter's eloquent and cogent statement leads to the inescapable conclusion that the mere possession of nuclear arms by any nation is morally indefensible.

The Second Vatican Council did not really respond to the thrust of Cardinal Ritter's challenge. The Council fathers made some attempt to answer the question but in the end left it unresolved. The Council states that the "defensive strength of any nation is considered to be dependent upon its capacity for immediate retaliation against an adversary. Hence this accumulation of arms, which increases each year, also serves, in a way heretofore unknown, as a deterrent to possible enemy attack." The Council goes on to concede that "many regard this state of affairs as the most effective way by which peace of a sort can be maintained between nations at the present time." But we are not told who are the "many" who regard the present state of affairs as "the *most* effective way" to maintain peace. Indeed the Council seems to contradict itself since in another place in the 2,500 word statement the Council fathers claim that "the arms race is an utterly treacherous step for humanity, and one which injures the poor to an intolerable degree."

There are some within the Catholic church who advocate

the total abolition of nuclear weapons even if this means unilateral disarmament. This naive and unrealistic approach is rejected, on the other hand, by many persons who feel that the use of nuclear weapons — at least as a deterrent — is required because the other side has comparable weapons.

Silence or confusion on the part of Catholics is most unfortunate — especially in view of the fact that Catholic tradition with respect to the elements of a just war is probably more highly developed than the theology of any other Christian or even religious body in the world. Christian theologians are obviously unable or unwilling to confront the consequences of accepting the moral imperative of Pope John and to some extent the Vatican Council that all modern and especially nuclear war is immoral. At least a few Christian theologians have sought to think the unthinkable and to respond to the question of whether Christian nations must allow annihilation rather than violate the fundamental rules of morality by participating in a war which would bring about the deaths of millions of persons. Father John C. Ford, S.J., a noted moralist, wrote in 1957 that if the alternative to the immoral use of atomic weapons were subjugation to an atheist regime or the extinction of the human race "the followers of Christ should abandon themselves to divine providence rather than forsake (Christian moral) imperatives." The majority Catholic opinion, however, was probably summed up by the English writer, Mr. E. I. Watkin, when he wrote: "I fear most Catholics are persuaded that the evil of worldwide subjection to Communist governments is so great that the deployment of *any* means indispensable for preventing it, even the worldwide slaughter and ruin of atomic warfare, is justifiable."

Mr. Watkin goes on to pose the fundamental question confronting all of us with these words:

> May it not be that God is inviting us to meet and defeat the challenge of modern materialism and competent secularism in all its forms, not only Marxist, but a supreme act of faith in His omnipotence which renounces methods of warfare which conscience plainly condemns?

An opinion expressly contrary to this has been eloquently stated by the distinguished Protestant theologian, Dr. Paul Ramsey. Dr. Ramsey in his volume *The Just War: Force and Political Responsibility* argues that the quality of life under a Communist regime and the suppression of religious freedom which could be anticipated in a Marxist state offer adequate reasons for Christians to use military means to prevent a Communist takeover of a neutral or of a Christian nation. This is without doubt a minority opinion and would appear to be contrary to the strong statements of the National Council of Churches and the World Council of Churches, both of which organizations appear to share the conviction that no interpretation of traditional Christian ethics of warfare can morally justify a nuclear clash.

If Christians are confused or undecided about how far they should go in declaring a war on nuclear war they have to realize that there are other distressing situations in the world which almost inevitably breed war. Mankind this year will spend more than five hundred billion dollars on arms. This means that humanity spends well over one billion dollars each day for arms and armaments. These enormous sums, unprecedented in the history of humanity, clearly suggest that war is becoming more likely because more nations are preparing for it. One can be cynical and state that in the 3,423 years of recorded history only 268 of these years have seen no war — as revealed in the book *The Lessons of History* by Will and Ariel Durant. But the modern preparation for war is worse in every way than any previous preparation in another generation. Today the expenses of nations arming themselves inevitably result in the worldwide situation where at least 800 million people are chronically malnourished. Christians in the developed nations find themselves bewildered and baffled at the thought that the industrialized nations are almost certainly helping more wars to be created by selling arms to the nations of the Third World. The United States is particularly culpable since it is the largest seller of arms with a total volume of sales in 1981 to approach 15 billion dollars.

It is overwhelmingly clear that the Soviet Union and the United States are like scorpions in a bottle which cannot move without inflicting massive damage on each other. Americans are weary of living out this contest which has taken on the aura of an international game in which the stakes are beyond human imagination. But the very concept of a "game" promotes the further concept that a gain for one side is inevitably a loss for the other. The game is senseless because both sides lose by "winning" and neither side can win except by stopping the "game."

Disarmament and the future of Salt II are very much in doubt at this time. Catholics have a very distinctive and unique role to play. They have an opportunity of surpassing importance and urgency —perhaps the most significant opportunity which Catholics have ever had in the history of the United States. If Catholics, aided by many others, can define and refine the wealth of their theological and moral traditions and articulate and act upon them in appropriate political ways they may be able to persuade the nation that it has a moral commitment to mankind to prevent, quite literally, the incineration of millions of human beings.

Chapter 14

A Future Seen Dimly

President Reagan wants to play tough, standing up to the air traffic controllers and standing up to the Soviet Union. While we will probably survive the disruption in airline schedules, the consequences of an American foreign policy confronting the Soviet Union pose a greater danger. This administration had made significant changes in American foreign policy, changes leading to a world that will be more secure for neither nations nor individuals.

In the short term, the administration's military policies increase the risk of military confrontation among nations and divert scarce resources from vital social services both here and abroad. The long-run effects of these policies may be even more profound.

This is more than merely a guns-versus-butter issue. Americans are concerned about the reduction in essential human services in Mr. Reagan's budget, necessitated, in part, by increased military spending. We need more butter, but it is the risks and dangers the guns create that jeopardize our future. We may pursue a mobile intercontinental ballistic missile at unprecedented costs to alleviate the so-called ICBM vulnerability problem. But doing so will foster the same strategic concern in the Soviet Union, which in turn, will have to address its military vulnerability problem and probably produce another dilemma for us.

Now the Reagan administration has decided to produce

First published in the The New York Times, August 14, 1981.

neutron warheads, supposedly to deter or halt a Soviet tank invasion of Western Europe. While the enhanced radiation weapon may be effective, can anyone doubt that if we produce it the Soviet Union will be far behind? The future for West European security may be even bleaker than it now appears, especially if American and Soviet leaders have less concern about using them than other tactical nuclear weapons.

Our conventional arms transfer policy in essence says to countries, "You are welcome to apply for American arms — at low cost or on credit — as long as you oppose the aspirations and ambitions of the Soviet Union." Neither human rights nor concerns for regional instability produced by local arms races plays a role in administration planning. We are guided by a single concern: the Soviet Union.

The two policies of increased military spending and arms sales will produce the same phenomenon: greater polarization of international relations. To be fair, the Reagan administration probably does not see the world simply as two armed camps flying the American and Soviet flags. Nevertheless, many of the policies we are adopting are rooted in this view of the world. This view has a significant self-reinforcing feature: as we encourage countries to ally themselves with one of the superpowers, we see the world more in terms of the United States versus the Soviet Union. And this feeds into the cycle and fosters a mythical need for still greater military spending and arms sales. We end up with a far more dangerous international environment.

We do not want a world in which a multitude of countries have stockpiles of atomic weapons. Yet the Reagan administration's policy against the spread of nuclear weapons contains little substance and does nothing to prevent the spread of fissionable materials. President Reagan's decision to support the Clinch River fast breeder reactor, for example, contributes to the development of international commerce in plutonium. By backing the breeder, which relies on plutonium fuel, the administration opens another avenue for diversion of this incredibly dangerous material to countries or terrorists. A mere five to ten kilograms, which is about the size of a baseball, is enough to build a bomb.

The administration does not take the spread of atomic weapons seriously enough, and this may be the president's grim legacy to history. The administration supports the repeal of the Symington Amendment, which restricts aid to countries seeking nuclear weapons; the administration is vigorously pursuing a nuclear cooperation agreement with Egypt that will allow the introduction of yet another nuclear reactor into the Middle East; the administration supports nuclear power in all its forms; the Administration has yet to support Senator John Glenn's call for a meeting of the nuclear supplier nations to adopt stricter controls.

It is a safe bet that in the absence of an effective policy against the spread of nuclear arms — one that prevents access to plutonium and enriched uranium — our world will be far less secure. Such a future we must at all costs avoid.

The importance of stepping back and looking at our foreign policy with a sense of the future can never be overemphasized. Only by examining the longer-term impacts of what the Reagan administration is doing can we understand the grave international damage it will do. President Reagan's policies are harmful in the short run because they de-emphasize human rights and support increased wasteful military spending. When we peer beyond his myopia, we see that if the Reagan administration's foreign policy promises a world in which human rights are of secondary or marginal importance, confrontation replaces cooperation and atomic explosives are everyday weapons to be brandished about and perhaps actually used. We can ignore the future only at our own peril.

Chapter 15

Military Funds Soar, Making Eisenhower's Warning United States Reality?

Only 21 years ago, President Eisenhower in a farewell broadcast to the nation warned his fellow citizens of an entirely new element in American experience — "the conjunction of an immense military establishment and a large arms industry."

In that year the Pentagon's entire budget was $44 billion. That is the exact amount President Reagan proposes to increase spending this year. His fiscal 1982 proposal was an astounding $221 billion; it has been reduced to $214 billion. For fiscal 1983, the budget authority proposal is $258 billion, a $44 billion increase that is larger than Germany's entire defense budget and almost the same as Britain's.

Has there been what Eisenhower called "unwarranted influence by the military-industrial complex"? Has the nation succumbed to what the last soldier-president called "the temptation to feel that some spectacular and costly action could become the miraculous solution to all current difficulties"?

Is it relevant to note that the secretary of defense was vice president and general counsel of Bechtel Corporation, a vast global supplier of arms systems and that the secretary of state was president of United Technologies, a corporation that is engaged in similar undertakings?

The new five-year defense plan released by the Pentagon

First published in the *National Catholic Reporter*, June 11, 1982.

May 30 seems to assume that the Kremlin is an implacable foe and that nothing but a massive buildup in arms by the United States and its allies will contain the Soviets. No mention is made that the stupendous military might of the United States was powerless to prevent the fall of the shah, the invasion of Afghanistan, the repression in Poland or the global agony that resulted from OPEC's quintupling the price of oil.

The 125-page Pentagon document makes clear that the U.S. policy to defeat the Soviet Union at every level — from localized insurgencies to nuclear war. It predicts that in the future, "combat against Soviet forces, and possibly Soviet-supplied forces, will be of greater intensity and longer duration...."

The new Pentagon strategy goes beyond President Carter's Directive 59, which focused U.S. nuclear strategy on attacks on specific military targets. The Reagan nuclear strategy calls on American forces to be able to "render ineffective the total Soviet (and Soviet-allied) military and political structure."

The new document, at least taken as a whole, appears to go beyond all previous threats or warnings to Russia. The armed forces are directed to develop nuclear as well as conventional weapons and strategies to invade and conquer parts of Eastern Europe as well as the Persian Gulf. The paper moreover directs U.S. forces to be ready to enter Southwest Asia even without an invitation from a friendly government in that part of the world.

To carry out these objectives, the Pentagon projects that by 1991 there should be 25 army divisions rather than the current 16, 632 long-range aircraft rather than the existing 304, and 483 airforce bombers rather than the current 376.

Simultaneous with the revelation of the new defense posture was the Pentagon proposal of a new deployment technique for the MX missile — the "dense pack." This proposal would apparently cluster about 100 MX missiles in hardened underground silos over a small area of up to 15 square miles. Nearby there would be built anti-ballistic missile (ABM) sites to provide the first line of defense against Soviet attacks.

Even if one accepts the case for a land-based MX missile, "dense pack" seems to violate the 10-year-old ABM treaty, which confines U.S. and Soviet ABM deployments to either the nation's capital or to one of its land-based missile complexes.

The ABM treaty, probably the most valuable SALT I ingredient, was agreed because both sides saw in 1972 that the condition of "mutual assured destruction deters both sides from initiating a nuclear war. Hence they agreed to refrain from employing elaborate anti-missile defense systems.

The opposition to these now clearly spelled out new military strategies proposed after 500 days of the Reagan administration, seems at best diffused. Those who are horrified at the insensate military posture of the United States are currently involved in activities related to the nuclear freeze.

It is uncertain whether the White House will get all it declares is necessary for national defense. The reality is that spending for the Pentagon creates a deficit, a deficit keeps interest rates high and high interest rates cripple the economies of the United States and of our allies in Western Europe.

Ironically, those who want to give $1.5 trillion to the Pentagon during the next five years are asking that social programs be slashed, that taxes be increased and that deficits remain or grow. They are thus, in the name of defending a society, undermining the economies of the United States and of all free world nations. They are proposing this at a time when U.S. economic growth is lower than in four decades.

President Reagan plans to increase military spending by 52.8 per cent between 1981 and 1986 in inflation-adjusted, constant dollars.

Recently the non-profit Council on Economic Priorities compared the economic performance of 13 major industrial nations during the past two decades and found that "those countries that spent a smaller share of economic output on the military generally experienced faster growth, greater investment and higher productivity increases."

Perhaps we should add a footnote to President Eisenhower's famous warning. It may be that the "unwarranted influence of the industrial-military complex" will not bring about a "miraculous solution to all current difficulties" but might instead lay the groundwork for a collapse of the basic economic structures of the western world.

Chapter 16

Bishops Must Challenge Just-War Theory

Will the U.S. Catholic bishops in their November meeting state that the first use of the nuclear weapon is immoral? The committee of bishops charged with drafting a nuclear warfare policy will apparently be urging precisely that position. It has become known that the five-member committee headed by Archbishop Joseph Bernardin of Cincinnati will urge the hierarchy to condemn the use of nuclear weapons in all instances except in that rare (and perhaps impossible) situation where the use of an atomic device is necessary to knock out a military installation in a nation which has already detonated a nuclear bomb on the United States or on one of its allies.

Some bishops at the November meeting may resist and reject this recommendation. They will note that a policy that removes the first use of the nuclear weapon cuts the heart out of the contention that for 37 years the threat of the use of nuclear weapons has presumably acted as a deterrent and has prevented the use of any of the 50,000 weapons now in the possession of the United States, the USSR, England, France and China.

Removing the first use of the nuclear weapon is, furthermore, a policy no U.S. president has ever agreed to. The essence of U.S. policy has been to have nuclear weapons in the triad — on the land, at sea and in the air — to warn the other side that a massive assault by conventional weapons might

First published in the *National Catholic Reporter*, July 2, 1982.

prompt a nuclear response from the United States and that a nuclear attack would certainly provoke a massive retaliation in kind.

The bishops will be asked to proclaim, therefore, a substantial repudiation of a fundamental plank of existing U.S. foreign policy. They will be asked to decide a point left open by Vatican II — whether a nation may possess nuclear weapons not in contemplation of their use but solely for the purpose of deterrence.

In a book published in 1970, *Vietnam and Armageddon* (Sheed and Ward), I urged that the Catholic church convene Vatican III to deal exclusively with this precise question: can traditional Catholic concepts of a just war permit the possession of nuclear weapons for the sole purpose of deterrence even though these weapons may never be licitly used either offensively or defensively? The late Cardinal Joseph Ritter raised this question at Vatican II, but the 3,500-word statement of the Council on War evaded the issue by stating that "many regard this state of affairs as the most effective way by which peace of a sort can be maintained between nations at the present time."

The council did not identify the "many" who contend that the "accumulation of arms, which increases each year, also serves, in a way heretofore unknown, as a deterrent to possible enemy attack." This limp and uncertain conclusion with respect to a very difficult point has always seemed to me to jar with Vatican II's demand that Christians look upon war with an "*entirely* new attitude" (emphasis added).

If the bishops this fall adopt the findings of their own committee, they can cite the long-held and uncontradicted Catholic teaching that no weapons may ever be used against population centers or civilian targets. The "no first use" policy will enjoy the support of those who feel that a ban on the unilateral use of nuclear weapons is only a clear and perhaps inexorable inference from what Vatican II said about nuclear warfare.

But many well-informed Catholics will openly reject the episcopal position. It will be called unrealistic, an undesirable intrusion into a political question and a challenge to a position held on a nonpartisan basis by every president since Harry Truman. Some patriotic Catholics will assert, moreover, that the bishops' version of nuclear morality is not "official" and hence not binding on America's 50 million Catholics.

In the explosion of controversy to come, the following points should be kept in mind:

1. The just-war theory or tradition has been open to the most serious challenge since at least the end of World War II as a whole, it is difficult, if not impossible under the norms for a just war that go back to St. Augustine, to justify the bombing of Dresden, much less Hiroshima and Nagasaki.

Consequently any appeal to the just-war theory to validate the obliteration of one million or more persons in Moscow or Leningrad seems to be impossible because the requirement of proportionality cannot be met. Even if, let us assume, the political takeover of Western Europe by the Kremlin is prevented by the use of nuclear bombs, can the desirable moral objective obtained justify the deaths of millions of civilians and the possible radioactive contamination of extensive areas for a long period of time?

2. If the bishops condemn the use of atomic weapons, the Catholic church will be officially at odds with the U.S. policy of containing Communism. It has been assumed that the Catholic church would continue to support a policy of containing that political system which by its nature opposes the practice of Catholicism.

A ban on the first use of nuclear weapons means logically that the Catholic church must advocate the strengthening of conventional methods of warfare to the point that under no circumstances would the United States use or even threaten to use nuclear weapons if our adversaries appear to be more powerful than we are.

It may eventuate, therefore, that the bishops, by becoming nuclear pacifists, will have to become hard-line proponents of substantially increased expenditures for the buildup of the armed forces in the areas of conventional warfare.

3. More and more of the American bishops are men who received their seminary training during and after Vatican II. The pronouncements of this ecumenical council mean more to these bishops than the controversies and issues that were current in the church and in the world from 1945 to 1965. The upheavals

of that period have yielded the stage to concerns about world hunger and nuclear arms control. These two topics are closely interwoven.

The attention of America's Catholic bishops is now on the complex topic of how the United States, the richest and possibly the most idealistic nation in the history of the world, can use its resources to rid the universe of the scourge of nuclear holocaust and feed those two billion people who in the next 18 years will be added to the 4.2 billion human beings who now reside in the global village.

Chapter 17

Superpowers Vie for Third World Arms Sales

In 1982 the nations of the world will spend about $600 billion on arms and armaments. In 1960 the total was $100 billion. The 1982 figure comes to an average of $110 for each of the 4.2 billion persons on earth.

A recent international study called "Common Security" reported that "world military expenditure is more than 12 times as great in real terms as it was 50 years ago; it is more than 28 times as great as it was in 1908."

The U.S. Arms Control and Disarmament Agency (ACDA) recently stated that for 1979 the developing nations spent $129 billion on defense, triple the cost of a decade earlier.

One of the basic reasons so many developing nations squander their resources on weapons is the inducements given to them by the two superpowers to become a client state. The sale of weapons has now become the prime instrument used by the United States and the USSR in their rivalry for the allegiance of the Third World.

Although the wholesale transfer of arms from Russia and the United States began in the 1940s, President Carter was the only chief executive to try to cut back on the export of weapons. Despite his efforts, the export of American weapons rose from $10.1 billion in the mid 1970s to a new high of $17.4 billion in 1980.

President Carter's policy was completely reversed by the

First published in the *National Catholic Reporter*, September 24, 1982.

Reagan White House. In July 1981, the Reagan administration proclaimed that "the United States...views the transfer of conventional arms...as an essential element of its global defense posture and an indispensable component of its foreign policy."

Pursuant to this policy, the value of foreign military sales proposed by President Reagan in his first year of office rose to $25.3 billion. The Reagan administration has furthermore created a warehouse for weapons. With $600 million available to create a stockpile of weapons for 1983, the result will be that the United States can rush arms anywhere in the world where a conflict breaks out.

The theory behind the massive sale of arms is to counter communism by making allies of those who purchase their weapons from the United States. The record shows, however, that the United States has been making friends with authoritarian dictatorships. Until the time of the Carter administration, aid and sales of military equipment had been extended to 28 of the 41 military-dominated governments in the world with records of violating the rights of citizens by arbitrary arrest, torture and summary execution. In the past two decades, the United States exported almost $27 billion worth of weapons to these 28 countries, and during the past three decades has trained 347,000 military personnel from these lands.

The facts about arms sales by the USSR are almost as frightening as those by the United States. In 1980 Soviet arms agreements totaled $14.9 billion. The sales from the three top suppliers in the West, the United States, France and England, came to $25 billion.

The presence of massive numbers of weapons around the world is likely to have consequences the horror of which can now hardly be imagined. The mere presence of these weapons will create regional rivalries. These weapons will be used to perpetuate authoritarian regimes or to overthrow military dictatorships. Even worse, weapons of all kinds will be acquired by theft or by purchase by terrorists of all ideological descriptions.

Although some have criticized the Carter administration as not zealous enough in following through on its pledges to cut back on arms sales, the Carter White House looks very admirable compared to what is transpiring now. The Reagan administration has asked Congress for the removal of the ban on arms sales for Argentina and Chile, has urged the repeal of the Clark amendment which prohibits military assistance to the anti-Marxist faction in Angola and has requested the overturn of the Symington amendment, which in effect outlawed aid to Pakistan until it pledged to refrain from developing nuclear weapons. The Reagan administration furthermore has sold military equipment to Jordan, to Peking and to Venezuela — the last a first for Latin America.

The world has been astonished at the intensity, the universality and the effectiveness of the nuclear freeze movement. If the advocates of a nuclear freeze turn their anger and their scorn on America's really horrifying role as the world's number one supplier of the instruments of death and destruction, could we witness a major modification of the U.S. policy on arms sales?

We have seen a real change in the Reagan White House as the result of massive protests against nuclear war by millions of people on both sides of the Atlantic. If the nuclear bomb is ticking, the explosion that can be anticipated from the global proliferation of conventional weapons cannot be far behind.

Chapter 18

1983 Target Turning Point for Arms Race

On November 2, a significant majority of some 18 million Americans cast their ballots in favor of a nuclear freeze. Despite the opposition of the Reagan administration and the Pentagon, the nuclear freeze is now a moral and political issue which will not go away. It could become a powerful issue in the 1984 presidential campaign. It could signal a new era in arms control in which the people as well as the professionals are involved.

The results of the nuclear freeze referendum are of special importance to those who followed closely the deliberations on nuclear warfare of the 300 U.S. Catholic bishops in Washington this month. The final statement of the bishops, expected in May 1983, will expressly endorse the idea of the nuclear freeze and indeed go beyond that to urge in the strongest terms the reduction and eventual elimination of all nuclear weapons.

The future of the nuclear freeze movement will be of enormous importance to those who agree with Pope John Paul II's statement in Madrid November 3 that the concentration of scientific effort on the development of nuclear weapons is a "scandal of our time."

Although the issue of nuclear arms is enormously complex, it is a sign of progress that the people of the United States have once again become directly involved in pressing to end the escalation of the arms race.

On two previous occasions the intervention of the people was effective. Worldwide panic and protest about atmospheric testing brought about the test ban treaty in 1963. Mothers demonstrating outside the White House protesting strontium

First published in the *National Catholic Reporter*, November 26, 1982.

in their children's milk induced President Kennedy to agree to sign a ban with the Soviets on all nuclear testing in the atmosphere.

The second occasion when the people of America became aroused about arms control centered on the antiballistic missile. All across the nation, people during the 1960s protested the presence in their communities of these devices designed to shoot down incoming Soviet missiles. The protest was so vehement and sustained that funding for the ABM from Congress became very uncertain. As a result, President Nixon agreed with the Soviets in SALT I to ban construction of the ABM.

The ABM treaty was an act of faith by both superpowers in the rationality of the other side. It was perhaps the greatest triumph for disarmament in the 37-year history of the nuclear arms race, and it would not have been accomplished except for a broad coalition of citizens who were opposed to what they properly felt was a needless expenditure of massive sums of money and, more important, a dangerous escalation of the nuclear arms race.

What should be the next step for those who on November 2 had a very significant victory at the polls? If normal conditions prevailed with respect to arms control, the answer would be to return to SALT II and seek its ratification. After all, this was the work of both Democratic and Republican presidents for a period of more than six years. The treaty was signed by the Soviets and by President Carter. Its ratification was postponed after the Soviet invasion of Afghanistan in December 1979.

It does not appear feasible, however, to revive SALT II, as President Reagan has regularly characterized that agreement as "fatally flawed." In a total contradiction, however, he has also said his administration would abide by the provisions of SALT II. The Reagan proposal called START bypasses the highly successful SALT process and confuses the entire strategic arms situation by initiating proposals never before introduced into nuclear arms negotiations.

The grim fact is that Reagan has at every moment of the nuclear age opposed any nuclear arms negotiations. He opposed the test ban treaty in 1963, the non-proliferation agreement in 1968, the suspension in 1969 of the manufacture of poisons for biological and chemical warfare, and the ban on the ABM in 1972.

There is, moreover, no indication that Reagan will alter his hitherto unaltered opposition to any form of arms control. In this situation, arms control advocates have a difficult role to play. They must go not to the president, but to the people with the hope that the people can arouse the president to be aware of the horrendous problems mankind faces in the nuclear threat.

Will the nuclear freeze movement, like the massive popular movement to end U.S. involvement in Vietnam, bring about an end to the nuclear madness between the superpowers? It could accomplish this objective if enough people learn the arcane vocabulary of the nuclear arms specialist and convince the people of the tragedy of continuing a situation which almost inevitably will result in a nuclear holocaust.

It is particularly encouraging to note that lawyers, following the example of physicians, are now deeply involved in seeking to evolve some resolution of the nuclear arms impasse. The Lawyers Alliance for Nuclear Arms Control (LANAC) is a well-organized group of attorneys with chapters in all the major cities of the country including Washington, D.C. Attorneys who belong to LANAC recognize that as members of the bar, they have unusual and unique qualities which equip them to be mediators in the struggle between those forces that have brought about that the United States now has 30,000 nuclear weapons in its possession.

It is to be hoped that lawyers will be the moral architects of those solutions which were embodied in SALT II but which now have the nuclear freeze movement as the only possible viable method by which the people of America can demand some reversal of the arms race.

The year 1983 may well be the turning point in the nuclear arms race. The Catholic bishops and indeed churches of all denominations all around the world will be speaking out as never before in the history of the nuclear age. If enough people are as determined as the one-fourth of the nation who voted for the nuclear freeze November 2, it may be that the year to come will see at least the end of the beginning in mankind's quest for deliverance from the possibility of a nuclear holocaust.

Chapter 19

Down to a "Yes" or "No" on the Deadly MX

Will the congress fund the most massive weapon of death ever devised by humanity and call it the "Peacekeeper"? The vote in Congress could go either way. As a result public opinion on this question will almost certainly be more important than it has been on nearly any issue considered by Congress during the past several years.

Common Cause, the 230,000-member citizens' lobby, has joined scores of organizations opposed to the placing of 100 missiles in a "dense pack" formation near Cheyenne, Wyoming. The struggle for at least $26 billion in funding for the MX will undoubtedly be a battle that will be titanic as well as momentous for the future of the world.

As proposed by President Carter in 1979, the MX was designed to counter the theoretical threat to the entire U.S. force of 1,052 land-based missiles by more accurate Soviet ICBMs. This perceived threat is the alleged window of vulnerability referred to as a certain menace by the Reagan administration but dismissed as nonexistent by knowledgeable arms control experts such as Paul Warnke, a negotiator for SALT II.

The MX is designed to be an improved version of the Minuteman III. But upon analysis the improvement is only marginal. The MX will not have added accuracy, but it will carry 10 warheads compared to only three for the Minuteman III. A later version of the MX is projected to be twice as accurate as the improved Minuteman III.

First published in the *National Catholic Reporter*, December 10, 1982.

Do these improvements justify the expenditure of a sum which after overruns and miscalculations could reach $60 billion? Is this increased survivability necessary in view of the thousands of nuclear arms the U.S. now possesses in its strategic bombers and its missile-launching submarines? Is an improved land-based third leg of the triad really necessary to provide a hedge against Soviet technical breakthroughs in anti-submarine warfare and air defense?

The Pentagon will be pressing hard to get the MX started. The lobby for this missile will undoubtedly be as intense as the successful White House effort that persuaded a Senate majority to vote in favor of a sale of $8.5 billion worth of AWACs to Saudi Arabia.

The arguments against the MX are almost as arcane as the arguments in its favor. Opponents note that each side's ICBMs have become so accurate that there is really no way to guarantee the survival of land-based missiles in fixed locations. Senator Henry Jackson (D-Wash.) has conceded that the MX when finally built would be invulnerable for only four years. As a result the retaliatory capacity of the MX can be secure only if the United States adopts a launch-on-warning policy — that is, the nation would launch its missiles during the short period between the time the attacking missiles are detected by surveillance satellites and the time they arrive at their targets.

The adoption of such a policy would decrease the vulnerability of the ICBMs but could sharply increase the danger that a nuclear war could be started by the United States because of a miscalculation that the USSR had launched nuclear weapons.

MX opponents also point to the fact that the Soviet Union would not be inclined to try to knock out every U.S. land-based missile because, even if this effort succeeded, the Soviets would be struck by a devastating counterattack by the U.S. long-range bombers and submarine-launched missiles.

Less persuasively perhaps, MX opponents argue that "dense pack" may violate the SALT II ban on constructing new, fixed ICBM launchers. MX opponents also argue that construction of the MX may lead to the need for an anti-missile ballistic system — which the United States agreed to abandon in SALT I.

The forces against the MX also dispute the wisdom of having the MX as a "bargaining chip." Such reasoning in the past has led to an escalation in the arms race and not to useful negotiations. Adversaries of the MX state, moreover, that even if one yields on the need for the MX, no basing mode has yet been discovered which would guarantee adequate survivability. Finally it is contended that the MX has first-strike capabilities and is therefore capable of introducing a destabilizing element into the nuclear balance.

President Reagan's nationally televised address November 22 in favor of the MX is no doubt only the first effort in a relentless administration drive to get the "Peacekeeper" funded. The White House will try to frighten the American people with the theoretical problem which *does* exist — the vulnerability of U.S. land-based ICBMs.

Spokespersons for the Pentagon will, moreover, consciously or otherwise, wrap the debate in technical language and exotic vocabulary. Oceans of ink will be spilled over the meaning of "fratricide, — the possibility of Soviet warheads that could land softly and thereby avoid fratricide and the feasibility of "pin-down" or high altitude detonations which would continue until all the missiles are destroyed in their silos.

To many all of this will seem like the science fiction fantasies of Buck Rogers or Rube Goldberg. Even the *New York Times* in an editorial condemning the MX November 24 conceded that "the technical issues are beyond us." But bafflement, mockery or derision are not appropriate now that the construction of the MX is down to a "yes" or "no" vote by 535 members of Congress.

It is a time for citizens to study, to be well informed and to discuss the issue knowledgeably. The most dangerous moment in the 37-year history of the nuclear arms race may be here. In addition to their solemn duties as citizens, American Catholics now have a sacred duty to carry out the recommendations of America's Catholic bishops with respect to the moral aspects of nuclear warfare.

Chapter 20

The Specter of Chemical Warfare

One of the most unbelievable items in the massive military buildup being urged on the Congress by the Reagan administration is a request for $158 million for nerve gas munitions and equipment. Last year Congress turned down a request for $54 million for this purpose, thereby refusing to end a 14-year moratorium on U.S. production of chemical weapons.

The abandonment by humanity of lethal biological and chemical weapons is possibly the greatest victory for arms control in the 20th century. World revulsion at the killings caused by poison gases in World War I led to the Geneva Protocol of 1925 which banned the use but not the manufacture of asphyxiating gases.

The United States signed this treaty June 17, 1925, but the United States Senate has never ratified it. Although, technically, the United States is not a party to the treaty, the United States on December 5, 1966, supported a United Nations general assembly resolution calling for strict observance of the Geneva Protocol.

In addition, President Nixon, November 25, 1969, asserted that the United States "reaffirms its oft-repeated renunciation of the first use of lethal chemical weapons." Nixon urged the Senate to ratify the Geneva Protocol forbidding the use of chemical weapons.

In 1976 President Ford initiated negotiations with the Soviet Union on a chemical weapons ban. In early 1980 the United

First published in the *National Catholic Reporter*, March 4, 1984.

States and the USSR had agreed on most of the points in a chemical disarmament treaty. Unfortunately, the Carter administration was not able to finalize these arrangements. The Reagan administration has refused to reopen bilateral chemical disarmament talks with the Soviet Union.

Congress has been resisting chemical weapons for almost a decade. In 1975 Congress twice refused funding to build a chemical weapons plant in Arkansas. It also forbade the production of chemical munitions unless the president certified that such production was essential to the national interest. Neither Ford nor Carter ever made such a determination.

In 1982 the House killed the $52 million requested for chemical weapons by a 251-159 vote. The Senate agreed to the expenditure, 49-45. The measure died in conference. The Council for a Livable World can probably take more credit than any other peace organization for the defeat of appropriations for chemical warfare. The council demonstrated to the satisfaction of a House majority that the United States now possesses a stockpile of chemical shells adequate to supply all U.S. and NATO forces for 45 days of continual chemical warfare in Europe.

The Reagan administration continues to insist that the Soviet Union is using chemical weapons in Afghanistan and Indochina. Even if this is so, it does not follow that the United States should acquire weapons it does not need and which Britain, West Germany and the Scandanavian nations do not want on their soil.

Those who are eager to do all possible to stop the 98th Congress from financing the spectacular escalation in the Pentagon budget being aggressively advanced by the Reagan administration will have to concentrate on attempts to cut back the massive sums proposed for items such as the MX missile and the B1 bomber.

But the $158 million requested for weapons to produce psychiatric and neurological disorders to millions of civilian victims constitutes a specific and comprehensive target eminently worthy of the efforts of those who want the United States not to manufacture chemical weapons but to push for a comprehensive ban on their development and production.

Chapter 21

Catholic Educators and a New Vision of the World

A new moment in the history of American Catholicism has arrived. Our bishops have solemnly criticized and repudiated the basic premises of our nation's foreign policy. Hierarchies around the world have substantially agreed with them. The National Council of Churches which represents most Protestant bodies has endorsed the bishop's statement. And the promise and the prestige of America's 52 million Catholics might well be at a new high.

But all of this brings uneasiness. In March 1982, Father Richard McCormick, S.J., a distinguished moral theologian, saw this coming and wrote in Theological Studies:

> The religious leadership in the United States — especially Catholic — is on a collison course with the United States government. That just might be the best thing to happen to both in a long time.

The message of the bishops about nuclear war is clear. It is not essentially different from what the 2,300 Catholic bishops said in Vatican II in 1965. But it is for us now more imperative because the pastoral not only condemns the use of nuclear weapons but makes the continued posession of them by our

Address at the 81st Annual Convention of National Catholic Education Association, April 24, 1984, Boston, Massachusetts.

nation contingent on the presence of specific plans to phase them out.

The pastoral has shaken us. For decades Catholics have sought to portray themelves as even more patriotic than other Americans. But now we are trying to adjust to a situation which places us in fundamental opposition to a core doctrine of America's foreign policy. We are chagrined that we have hitherto not seen or certainly have not acted on the moral unacceptability of our nation threatening to use levels of nuclear destruction which cannot be justified by any interpretation of traditional Catholic teaching.

We are all experiencing a great awakening. We have guilt for our previous blindness and silence. And we have ever deepening angst and anxiety as to what we should do personally and collectively about the policies which our government has adopted and which we by our tradition and by our conscience cannot accept.

The struggle against our government has just begun. The questions will become more complex and the challenges more demanding. As Christians we have openly repudiated the use and the threat of use of nuclear weapons. The consequences of that courageous commitment are just beginning to become clear to us.

There is no point in trying to minimize the break, the rupture which Catholics have made with the policies of nuclear deterrence followed by the United States. The repudiation is clear. We can try to postpone the showdown by talking about the necessity of deterrence or by the requirements of national security. But we will have nothing but guilt late on if now we refuse to admit that we are being asked by the Church of God to take an attitude toward nuclear war which will make severe demands on the way we think, live and act.

The new moment in the history of Catholicism in America which we are now experiencing has consequences not only for our own sanctification and salvation but also quite literally for the entire future of the world. All of mankind, frightened by the possibility — even the probability — of a nuclear war, is looking with great expectation to the Catholic church in America which is now supported by the vast majority of religious groups in the United States. Could the Catholic church, one wonders, become the most influential peace church of all times?

I have a vision and a dream. I dream and pray that 50 years from now historians will look back and see a world that has set aside or greatly curtailed the possession of nuclear weapons and be able to trace the nuclear disarmament of the world to the moral initiatives of Catholic leaders in America. Would it not be marvelous for the church and for mankind if history could record that it was the voice and vision of 300 Catholic bishops in America, echoed and amplified by the 961,000 nuns, 413,000 priests and 783,000,000 laypersons all over the globe, that induced the nations to abandon nuclear weapons?

I have a further vision that 50 years from now it will be clear that it was the teachers and the 3 million students in Catholic schools of America that led the moral revolution which culminated in the elimination of nuclear weapons from the arsenals of mankind. That vision is not impossible because Catholic theology has the most developed moral system in the world, and Catholic schools in America may be the best organized and most visionary of such institutions in the world.

How can these twin visions be realized? only by the most intense rethinking of America's role in the world and the rejection of many of the misconceptions which have led the United States and the world to what may well be the most dangerous point in the 30 year history of the nuclear arms race.

A rethinking of America's role in the world requires that attention be given to several crucial global developments among which are the following:

1. In the 16 years before the year 2000 some 2 billion more human beings will be with us in the human family. The world population will grow from 4.6 billion to 6.4 billion. Virtually no planning of any kind is going on to provide for this vast number of our new brothers and sisters. Today 800 million persons are chronically malnourished. Unless something dramatic is done that figure will be tragically higher in the year 2000.

   Consider what will happen in 1985. Eighty million infants

will be born; 25 million of these will die before they are 5 years old.

The United States contains only 5 percent of the world's population but consumes some 40 percent of the world's resources.

In 1974 the United States at a world conference on food in Rome solemnly pledged that "within a decade no child will go to bed hungry." That pledge has not been redeemed.

The Presidential Commission on Hunger, chaired by Sol Linowitz, recommended that the alleviation of hunger become one of the principal objectives of our foreign policy. Clearly the possibility of global famine is one of the most dangerous threats to our national security.

2. Vatican II mandated that all Christians think of war "with an entirely new attitude." That statement reflected the thinking of Pope John's electrifying message *Pacem in Terris* issued on Easter Sunday in 1963.

How does "an entirely new attitude" towards war deal with the incredible fact that this year the amount the world spends on arms and armaments has escalated to $660 billion — almost $2 billion per day? There is no other conclusion except that this vast expenditure is virtually the cause of the starvation of children and the continued illiteracy of millions of adults.

The Second Vatican Council noted that "while extravagant sums are being spent for the furnishing of ever new weapons an adequate remedy cannot be provided for the multiple miseries afflicting the whole modern world."

3. Catholics in a special way must rethink the relationship of the United States to Latin America. One half of the people in the world who call themselves Catholic — 350 million — reside in Latin America. Since Vatican II, Medellin and Puebla, Catholics in Latin America have as never before been striving to liberate themselves from political and economic tyrannies. U.S. foreign policy in Central America, however, has overlooked this development and has treated the situation as an East-West conflict.

Again the bishops of the United States have condemned

the policies of our country. With unusual insistence the hierarchy has denounced the furnishing of U.S. military assistance to Central America.

Can we again have the vision and the dream that 50 years from now historians will be able to say that it was Catholic leaders in the United States who changed the policy of their country from one that assisted authoritarian and military regimes to one that fostered political and economic liberation?

We know that many of our priorities are fundamentally different from the priorities embraced by the foreign policy of our nation. We want to be courageous. But what do we do? We can educate and we can pray, but we have a deepening feeling that this is not enough. We see the madness in the arms race and the agony in Central America and we want to do something.

We should nurture these feelings as graces that come directly to us from God. Anger at injustice, rebellion against policies of our government and the desire to change immoral practices are inspirations of the Holy Spirit. They are like the moral outrage that inspired the abolitionists to organize around the year 1800. Those reformers might have been discouraged if they knew that slavery would not be abolished until 1865. But the resistance and the ridicule never caused them to doubt the need for abolition and the inevitability of its happening.

As the controversy over the possession of nuclear weapons becomes more intense, it will be suggested that the church and its servants must not become too closely involved in secular matters. That approach will almost certainly be advanced when the Catholic bishops in late 1984 issue the first draft of their pastoral on economic and social justice. Those who hate the message will seek to silence the messenger. But Christians who by the gospel itself must have a preferential option for the poor will recognize that if we run away from the world we run away from God.

Pierre Teilhard de Chardin, S.J., said it well when he wrote that "our faith imposes on us the right and the duty to throw ourselves into the things of the earth."

Vatican II, the Synods of 1971 and 1974 and indeed every

statement of the highest authorities of the church over the last
generation have made it clear that the strengthening of faith
and the promotion of justice go together. They form the one
single mission of the church.

The 32nd General Congregation of the Society of Jesus put it
well:

> ...the way to faith and the way to justice are inseparable
> ways. It is up this undivided road, this steep road, that the
> pilgrim church must travel and toil. Faith and justice are
> undivided in the gospel....

It is a solemn moment for the church — in America and
around the world. Humanity may be on the brink of killing
millions of people and contaminating the atmosphere with
radioactive substances for the rest of recorded history. The
church has warned mankind in unusual and unprecedented
ways. The church in all its majesty and beauty is begging to be
heard by the world.

We feared until recently that we were living at a time of the
church's unqueening. But now the eyes of the entire world are
looking to the church with the hope that the church's courage
and commitment may lead to a radical change in the arms race.

The world is looking particularly to the Catholic church in
America for leadership. Only 6.6 percent of the world's 783
million Catholics live in America, but the United States has 11
percent of the world's nuns and 14 percent of the world's
priests. It is this church that has suddenly commanded the
attention of the world. It has embarked on an uncharted pilgrimage. It has challenged the morality of some of the basic
political premises of the nation. It has become like the prophets
of the Old Testament.

What are the next steps for the church in America? The
answer to that question depends to a great extent on the
Catholic educators of America. If they reorient their curricu-
lum, reshape the thinking of their students and bring forth a
new generation of citizens who think with the church in its
anguish for humanity, it could be that the foreign policy of our
country could be altered to conform to the principles of basic

morality. But if Catholic educators fail to see the vision or follow the dream now before all of us no one can fail to see the tragedies that could befall the church and the nation.

This is a unique moment in our lives, in our church and in the mission of the National Catholic Education Association.

In the recent past a distinguished group of Jewish Americans established a private commission to study the question of whether or not American Jews during the time of the holocaust could have done more to prevent or mitigate the tragedies that happened to the Jewish people at that time. The findings of the commission suggest that more could have been done but was not done.

Will a similar commission 50 years from now come to the painful conclusion that American Catholics in the 1980's could have done more to curb the nuclear arms race but that they did not?

Silence on difficult issues can generally be rationalized and justified rather easily. Catholics were all too silent about the immorality of nuclear war from the time that it was condemned by Vatican II in 1965 to the publication of the bishop's pastoral in 1983. The world is now waiting for Catholics who constitute only 18 percent of the total population of the Earth to rise up and to make the world safe from nuclear conflagration.

Chapter 22

...Or Exhortation to Consider Abortion above All?

The August 9 statement from the National Conference of Catholic Bishops (NCCB), issued by its president, Bishop James W. Malone, on religion and politics builds upon but does not substantially differ from statements on political responsibility which the bishops have been issuing at least since 1976.

As in 1976, the bishops make several disclaimers concerning their role in the political process. They do not want to "take positions for or against political candidates." Nor do they want to create a voting bloc of Catholics. Indeed, they do not want religion to be an issue in the campaign. "It would be regrettable," the bishops state, "if religion, as such, were injected into a political campaign through appeals to candidates' religious affiliations and commitments."

In a statement issued earlier in 1984, the bishops insisted once again that voters should "examine the positions of candidates on the full range of issues, as well as the person's integrity, philosophy and performance."

The bishops see the need for dialogue. They concede that some do not "share our moral convictions." Because of this, the bishops speak out "to make a religiously informed contribution to the public policy debate in our pluralistic society." They do so because they feel "the need to join the public policy debate in a way which attempts to convince others of the rightness of our positions."

First published in the *National Catholic Reporter*, August 31, 1984.

The episcopal statement expresses the bishops' interests in the several issues on which they testified to both the Democratic and Republican platform committees; these issues include nutrition, human rights, housing, education, health care for the poor and civil rights. But the bishops place "particular emphasis on abortion and nuclear war." These two issues are different. The reason: the immorality of the "direct taking of innocent human life" by abortion and the "direct attacks on noncombatants in war" are the "constant moral teaching of the Catholic church."

The distinction is clear enough, but what is not clear is whether elected officials' votes on abortion and nuclear war are to be treated differently by voters. It would appear that this is not intended because it is still urged that voters make a survey of the "full range of issues."

What is unclear, however, is the thrust of the following concept, which had never been used by the bishops before:

> We reject the idea that candidates satisfy the requirements of rational analysis in saying their personal views should not influence their policy decisions: the implied dichotomy — between personal morality and public policy — is simply not logically tenable in any adequate view of both.

Time magazine August 20 felt that these words were "obviously referring to abortion." This is not clear. The norm could also apply to votes regarding nuclear war, abortion or the various other issues the bishops mentioned.

It is difficult to identify any "candidates" who would fit the description in the episcopal statement. All candidates and incumbents openly admit that they have personal views which they try to insert into public policy. But most, if not all, legislators would also agree that there are occasions when legislators have the right and even the duty not to impose their views on others.

The constitutional amendment to prohibit the sale and use of all liquor might well have been such an attempt. The Reverend Jerry Falwell recently conceded in a televised discussion with me that the imposition of the 18th amendment by certain Protestant groups was a mistake.

If the comment about personal views and public morality is intended to apply to Catholic legislators voting on Medicaid funds for abortion, what are the implications?

About one-third of the Catholic members of Congress vote to permit public funds for abortions under Medicaid. The Congress several years ago adopted a policy of not funding Medicaid abortions, but votes on this question keep recurring.

The reasoning of those who vote to permit funding abortion is as follows:

1. Although the United States Supreme Court in 1980 in a five-four vote sustained the constitutionality of a federal ban on Medicaid funding for abortion, the arguments in the powerful and eloquent dissent are persuasive. The views in that dissent are concurred in by the court's one Catholic, Justice William Brennan, and the court's one black, Justice Thurgood Marshall.

2. Denying funding for poor women is perceived by millions of people to be unfair and violative of equal protection. This policy is perceived as denying a benefit to poor persons, who are denied their right under the Constitution to obtain a legal termination of a pregnancy.

Practicing and devout Catholics in the Congress are divided on this question. Congresswoman Claudine Schneider (R-R.I.) votes for federal funding for abortion, while Congresswoman Lindy Boggs (D-La.) votes against. Congressman Tom Harkin (D-Iowa) votes to allow funding; Congressman James Oberstar (D-Minn.) votes against funding. Senator Patrick Leahy (D-Vt.) votes to fund Medicaid abortions, while Senator Thomas Eagleton (D-Mo.) votes against funding.

3. Many Catholics feel uneasy about the contention that they are imposing their view of abortion on others. For Catholics, the immorality of abortion is very clear. For millions of Americans, however, the question is not that clear. The fact that 1.5 million abortions will take place in 1984 makes manifest the divergent views on this topic.

Should Catholic legislators feel impelled to give some deference to a point of view contrary to their own? In hearings some years ago, before the House Judiciary committee, the Catholic spokespersons were clear in their opposition to abortion. The spokespersons for the National Council of Churches were clear on the opposite side; they wanted to have the law continue to allow each woman to follow what her conscience, counseled by her physician and her family, told her to do.

Catholics in Congress who vote to allow Medicaid funds for abortion desire not to penalize or punish the millions of women for whom the National Conference of Churches speaks.

Some Catholics in Congress feel a question of religious freedom is involved in the way Congress votes on funding abortions. The Declaration on Religious Freedom of the Second Vatican council does not, of course, speak directly about what Catholics should do about abortion and the law. But the thrust of that enormously important document is to discourage force and coercion of any kind. Section 10 of the declaration contains these words:

> It is therefore completely in accord with the nature of faith that in matters religious, every manner of coercion on the part of men should be excluded.

To the militant pro-life advocates, these considerations are not persuasive. But Christian civility suggests that Catholic legislators who seek to cast a well-informed vote on a troubled issue should not be scoffed at or abused or categorized as disloyal to their religion.

One of the possibly major developments in the statement issued by Bishop Malone is the linking of abortion and nuclear war. Although the bishops do not want to "take positions for or against political candidates," the implications of their emphasis on nuclear war and a political order may be far-reaching. The statement opposes any "deterrence policies (which) would directly target civilian centers or inflict catastrophic damage." Those who seek to categorize Catholic legislators as "pro-life" or "pro-abortion" must also extend the equivalence of this identification to those who vote for every measure to escalate the arms race.

If a member of Congress votes for the MX, against the nuclear freeze, in favor of extending nuclear weapons to space, can he or she be deemed to be in violation of the essential principles set forth in the bishops' pastoral? Or is this "too political" an interpretation of the principles in the message of the National Conference of Catholic Bishops?

And if it is inappropriate to measure the votes of a member of Congress against the moral norms on nuclear war set forth by the hierarchy, then why is it appropriate to use episcopal statements to condemn a Catholic legislator who, on the basis of several moral considerations, votes to permit Medicaid funding of abortion?

The NCCB statement is useful. It discusses a difficult topic with as much clarity as is probably attainable. It will not solve all the moral dilemmas the electorate must face before November 6. But it can be hoped that it will not cause unnecessary problems.

History may well record gratitude for the Catholic community's leadership in seeking to protect unborn life. It is difficult to exaggerate the enormity of the problem. Recently, a Johns Hopkins survey estimated that 55 million abortions take place each year — 45 million of them in the Third World. The evil of abortion has infected many if not most Catholic countries. It is a problem that cannot be solved without massive education and a sharp reversal in public opinion.

But the evil of abortion does not relieve the American voter from the need for a well-informed, sophisticated approach to the "full range of issues" before the country at this time. If a legislator votes against Medicaid funding for abortion but votes regularly against most of the principles advocated by the bishops in their pastoral on nuclear war and in their testimony to the platform committees, can a vote for such a legislator be squared with an evaluation of the "full range of issues"?

In a 1979 statement on political responsibility for the 1980s, the Catholic bishops recognized that "our efforts in this area are sometimes misunderstood." They went on to state that the "church's participation in public affairs is not a threat to the political process or to genuine pluralism, but an affirmation of their importance."

Voters have very complex problems to resolve before November 6. The Catholic bishops of America have made clear that, in the words of Pope Paul VI, "the Christian has a duty to take part in the organization and life of political society." The bishops themselves have fulfilled that responsibility, as can be seen in the 487-page compendium of statements of the U.S. Catholic bishops on the political and social order from 1966 to 1980. It is hoped that the Catholic voters of America will follow their leadership and their counsel.

PART IV

Civil Rights

Chapter 23

The Reagan Administration and Civil Rights: The First Thousand Days

A counterrevolution in the area of civil rights has been launched in the 34 months of the Reagan Administration. For the first time the bipartisan consensus that has existed in civil rights since at least the Eisenhower Administration has been fragmented.

This development was not unpredictable since Mr. Reagan has always been opposed to the government and the law establishing and enforcing goals of equal opportunity. In 1964 he opposed the enactment of the Federal Civil Rights law; only 6 Republican Senators and 34 Republican Members of the House agreed with that position. Mr. Reagan, moreover, also opposed the fair housing bill proposed in 1966 in California. In 1980 he insisted that the Republican platform adopted in Detroit disapprove of busing for the purposes of racial integration and ban quotas designed to increase the number of minorities in schools or businesses.

The whole world is watching to see the extent to which the long held consensus on civil rights can be harmed. *The Economist*, a conservative British weekly that supports the president, noted as early as September 1981 that the Reagan administration was seeking to alter something fundamental in civil rights. *The Economist* predicted that the results would have immense repercussions all around the world since many nations have

First published in *America*, September 24, 1983.

written into their own law the civil rights laws enacted by the Congress in the 1960's.

The moral dimensions are, of course, obvious. The Second Vatican Council in its pastoral on "The Church in the Modern World" has these striking words: "With respect to the fundamental rights of the person, every type of discrimination, whether social or cultural, whether based on sex, race, color, social condition, language or religion, is to be overcome and eradicated as contrary to God's intent." This section is clearly an endorsement of legislation since it refers to an issue of public morality and calls for the "eradication" of any form of discrimination.

It is not easy to pinpoint the precise premises on civil rights on which the Reagan administration operates. In reaction to the vehement and almost daily criticism of the 165 public interest groups that make up the Leadership Conference, spokesmen for the Reagan administration have retreated from their position and altered their premises. But the core position of the Reagan justice department appears to be an insistence that a specific intent to discriminate be demonstrated before relief is granted and that nothing may be ordered or even permitted by the law which by affirmative action takes benefits away from members of the majority. These two positions are at odds with the statutory and decisional law that has developed over the past generation. But the assistant attorney general for civil rights, William Bradford Reynolds, justifies them by referring to the 1980 Republican platform. Civil rights activists are surprised and saddened by such a justification, since up to the time of the Reagan administration it had always been assumed that the enforcement of civil rights was an issue above politics and one that derived from the post-Civil War amendments to the Constitution and the manner in which the Congress and the courts have implemented these guarantees.

No one denies that there are difficult questions as to the extent to which affirmative action can be employed without bringing about reverse discrimination. But the Reagan justice department is opposed even to voluntary agreements by which minority workers can be given a certain preference for the duration of a specific period of time. Such an arrangement was approved in 1979 by the U.S. Supreme Court, in a 5-to-2 decision, *United Steelworkers v. Weber.* Brian Weber, a white worker, claimed that he was discriminated against by a plan collectively bargained for by his union and his employer that reserved for black employees 50 percent of the openings in a craft training program until the percentage of black craft workers in the plant was commensurate with the percentage of blacks in the local labor force. The court held that this voluntary approach did not violate Title 7 of the Civil Rights Act of 1964. The dissent of Justice William Rehnquist and Chief Justice Warren Burger argued that Congress intended to forbid all voluntary race-conscious affirmative action. It is that dissent that the Justice Department has now made into its official and vigorously defended position. The Justice Department is now seeking to impose that point of view in a New Orleans case where the lower court had approved a voluntary race-conscious arrangement to increase the number of minorities in the police force.

The doctrinaire condemnation by the Justice Department of all color-conscious distinctions in employment has caused extensive confusion among employers, government officials and labor leaders, all of whom desire to redress racial imbalance by remedies that provide not rigid quotas but attainable goals and targets. In many industries programs agreed to in good faith to utilize race-conscious affirmative action have now been abandoned or put on hold.

If the Justice Department is convinced that all affirmative action plans based on race-conscious considerations are wrong it could, of course, ask the Congress to make that clear. It has not attempted to do so, knowing that Congress is not likely to reverse the findings of the Weber decision or condemn the vast array of legal and administrative techniques designed to redress massive discrimination in the past. Indeed Congress would have to condemn years of work by the Equal Employment Opportunity Commission and other federal agencies that have carefully worked out plans to alter the colorblind attitudes that have resulted in the denial to minorities of their right to promotion and seniority. Congress is not likely, in other words, to set aside the positive and very successful techniques discovered by federal agencies to carry out the objectives of those monumental civil rights laws overwhelmingly enacted by the Congress on a nonpartisan basis. For Congress knows that the existence of pervasive discrimination based on race can be corrected only by sophisticated techniques of recognizing race for benign purposes and using color-consciousness to rectify patterns of discrimination in the past.

Despite this fact the Justice Department continues to deny or to restrict the applicability of affirmative action to housing, education, employment and other areas in which the federal government has long maintained a vigorous program to bring about desegregation.

Why the Reagan administration and the Justice Department continue to be adamant in pressing for a position not authorized by Congress or the courts is not entirely clear. Some extreme conservatives who have access to decision makers in the administration no doubt want to resist or reverse racial gains. The intense pressure on the administration to stop busing, furthermore, has apparently prompted the administration to develop legal principles for that area which logically they have to extend to other situations. The commitment, moreover, of continued opposition to the Equal Rights Amendment may require in the mind of administration spokesmen that all sex-conscious and race-conscious distinctions be disowned. But whatever the cause for the reversal by the Reagan administration of convictions previously held on a bipartisan basis, the results as seen by the civil rights community have been catastrophic.

The negative attitude of the administration toward curbing discrimination in housing typifies the reluctance to use the law to bring about equality of opportunity. In 1980, the House passed a bill tightening up the porous 1968 Fair Housing bill. The measure failed in the Senate. Civil rights activists thought that Samuel Pierce, the Secretary of Housing and Urban Development and the only black person in the Cabinet, might take advantage of the extensive work already done on the Fair Housing bill and move a bill banning bias in the sale or rental of housing. But it was not until mid-1983 that the Reagan administration finally sent a fair housing measure to Congress. It was, however, a bill that was too weak to gain the support of even the Republicans who had endorsed a stronger measure sponsored by the Leadership Conference and filed by Senator Charles Mathias (R., Md.). That means, in effect, that it is unlikely that any fair housing bill will pass the 98th Congress.

There are comparable developments on other issues. The White House withheld its endorsement of the Voting Rights Act until it was obvious that it was going to clear the Senate. The administration has filed a brief in the Supreme Court reversing prior policy and declaring that Title 9 of the 1972 Education Act that bans sex bias applies only to those programs specifically funded by the federal government. Grove City College in Pennsylvania claimed freedom from federal regulations because it receives no government money except the federal aid which its students receive. To the astonishment of Senator Robert Dole (R., Kan.) and many others, the Solicitor General has agreed with Grove City College. If he prevails, the result will be that the ban on sex discrimination will apply to only 4 percent of the $13 billion which goes annually to higher education. Again the administration could easily ask the Congress to clarify its intent if, as is claimed, the intent of Congress is ambiguous. But, as in the case of Bob Jones University, the Administration argues for a narrow view of civil rights without asking the Congress to broaden the scope and coverage of the law in question. The result is that inevitably the administration appears to be taking the side of those who do not want the federal government to broaden the opportunities for minorities or for women.

In one instance, however, the Justice Department has elected to endorse an expansive view of a federal law. Elizabeth Hishon spent seven years as an attorney in the Atlanta firm of King and Spalding, the former firm of Griffin Bell, Attorney General in the Carter Administration. Mrs. Hishon was not granted partnership in the firm and will argue her case before the United States Supreme Court in the near future. Her former firm will argue that the Civil Rights Act reaches corporations but not partnerships which, it is claimed, are by nature private, almost familial. The Justice Department has agreed with Mrs. Hishon, for reasons which seem inconsistent with its approach in comparable matters.

The titanic and unprecedented struggles going on between the civil rights community, as represented by the Leadership Conference, and the administration have been obscured by the battles between the President and the U.S. Commission on Civil Rights. This tiny agency with a budget of $13 million has done its duty and denounced the deviations from accepted and sound civil rights practice by the Reagan administration. The White House was so incensed that for the first time in history a president has removed three of the commissioners and named their replacements. The legal and political impasse that has resulted has tended to take the focus off the central questions of policy differences between the administration and the civil rights activists.

The damage being done to the enforcement of civil rights can be documented by ever more abundant evidence. Here are just a few instances:

1. In every year prior to the Reagan administration between 20 and 32 actions were brought by the Justice Department to enforce the federal fair housing laws. As of April 1983, only 5 cases had been filed under the Reagan administration.

2. The White House has cut the staff at the Department of Labor's Office of Federal Contract Compliance Programs by 50 percent.

3. According to the U.S. Civil Rights Commission, at the U.S. Department of Agriculture "civil rights enforcement has come to a virtual standstill."

4. The Justice Department has consistently refused to support the use of busing as a desegregation tool in any context. It has also advocated that federal courts be deprived of their power to employ busing as a remedial device.

5. In fiscal year 1982 over $196 million went to programs for school desegregation efforts and for the Women's Educational Equity Act. The administration desires to spend only $6.7 million on these programs in 1984.

The essential differences between the administration's approach to civil rights and that of the Leadership Conference may become difficult to discern in the months prior to the 1984 election. The administration continues to claim that it is enforcing civil rights vigorously. The Attorney General William French Smith recently blamed the constant criticism of the administration's approach to civil rights as "irresponsible journalism." He asserted that "some of these critics desire to create hostility among minority Americans. The motivation can only be political."

The critics of the administration will undoubtedly indulge in rhetoric of their own. They will tend to link charges of bias against blacks and women with criticism of the cutbacks in social programs for the poor and the handicapped. Careful and thoughtful evaluations of the legal and moral differences between the administration and the advocates of civil rights are not likely to be numerous in the popular press.

What is clear, however, is that the administration represents and may tend to exploit a deep feeling among many white Americans that they are in fact being denied opportunities in order that blacks can get ahead. This feeling may be largely unjustified. But it exists. It centers particularly on urban school systems, where the perception is often held that court-ordered integration has led to a decline in quality in the education offered.

The black community finds this feeling disappointing, even bewildering. They see it being used by the administration as a justification for sharply curtailing programs that have brought significant advances to the 26 million black citizens of America. It is not surprising, therefore, that black leaders feel abandoned and deserted. They see the reverses in policy and practice of the Reagan administration and they cry out for help. They have to recognize that the approach of the White House to civil rights will not change; the administration will continue to be opposed to affirmative action, preferential hiring targets, school desegregation by busing and expansive applications of federal civil rights machinery.

So the black community reacts with anger and even rage. Some of those feelings account no doubt for the support which the Reverend Jesse Jackson is receiving in some quarters for his contemplated race for the presidency.

Longtime white civil rights activists are also experiencing a uniquely difficult time. The fear exists that attitudes toward integration may be permanently altered and that even the desire to bring about equality of opportunity by law may be sharply decreased in the minds of millions. But again there seems to be little hope of changing the minds of those in the administration who are waging the counterrevolution against some of the fundamental policies of the civil rights revolution. But whites as well as blacks can be consoled that about $624 million will be spent next year in the major federal programs established to enforce civil rights. This sum, however, (slightly less in actual dollars than in the year before) cannot achieve desirable results if much of it is being spent to finance changes and reversals rather than advances and improvements in the enforcement of civil rights.

Blacks, women and the advocates of civil rights are clearly planning to make the country's commitment to equality of opportunity a central issue in the 1984 campaign. The administration will no doubt seek to make the changes it has brought about in civil rights policies and programs appear to be less radical than they are. The administration may seek to make its policies appear to be less harsh by accepting the idea of a national holiday for Dr. Martin Luther King. But the record of the administration has now been written. It is difficult if not impossible to undo the damage that has been done. Those who desire the "eradication" of prejudice, as called for by Vatican II, must seek to be well-informed so that in the forthcoming great national debate they can be calm and articulate defenders of the now challenged and threatened commitment that many years ago America made. That commitment pledged the United States government to use in creative ways the full force of its civil and criminal law to make real equality available for all Americans.

Chapter 24

Affirmative Action Under Attack

The Reagan administration has declared war on the concept of affirmative action in almost every one of its applications. In briefs filed in the U.S. Supreme Court the Justice Department has claimed that the city of Detroit may not constitutionally follow a plan of hiring an equal number of black and white persons for Detroit's police force until the number of blacks in the force is 50 percent. The assistant attorney general in charge of civil rights, William Bradford Reynolds, insisted that this plan discriminates against whites and is based on unconstitutional "quotas." On January 9th the Supreme Court declined to review the Detroit case, thus letting stand a lower court decision upholding the legality of the Detroit plan, but a similar case involving fire fighters in Memphis is still pending. But the administration will continue to pursue its conviction that affirmative action is neither required by nor consistent with the Constitution.

It is difficult to understand why the Reagan administration is so adamantly opposed to affirmative action. Nor is it possible to perceive any alternative it offers. In a recent debate with Mr. Reynolds I, and even some of the audience in the conservative Heritage Foundation where the debate was held, had difficulty in comprehending where Mr. Reynolds stood on the key Supreme Court decisions on affirmative action.

Affirmative action was born as a result of the Civil Rights Law of 1964. Implementing the purposes and spirit of that law,

First published in *America*, February 4, 1984.

federal agencies tried to make it clear that employers should reach out to minorities by "affirmative action." Their mandate was to bring the number of minorities in their work force more or less up to the percent of minorities in the local community. Goals, targets and timetables became the watchwords of officials at the Equal Employment Opportunity Commission and the Department of Labor as these agencies sought to rectify the thousands of situations where minorities had obviously been discriminated against for a long time. The term "quota," used benignly or otherwise, has been generally avoided.

President Johnson explained the purpose of his Executive Order 11246 in a speech at Howard University in 1965: "You do not take a person who, for years, has been hobbled by chains and liberate him, bring him up to the starting line of a race and then say, 'You are free to compete with all of the others.'"

Guidelines issued in 1972 by the Department of Health, Education and Welfare made it clear that Executive Order 11246 requires two things: 1) nondiscrimination or "the elimination of all existing discriminatory conditions whether purposeful or inadvertent" and 2) "affirmative action," which requires "the employer to make additional efforts to recruit, employ and promote qualified members or groups formerly excluded."

Professional and business groups have responded conscientiously and sometimes courageously to the challenges of affirmative action. Universities and others proudly proclaim that they are "affirmative action employers." The concept has entered the marketplace and has been accepted as fair and desirable.

The American Association of University Professors explained the concept of affirmative action in these words in 1973: "What is sought in the idea of affirmative action is essentially the revision of standards and practices to assure that institutions are in fact drawing from the largest marketplace of human resources in staffing their faculties and a critical review of appointment and advancement criteria to ensure that they do not inadvertently foreclose consideration of the best qualified persons by untested presuppositions which operate to exclude women and minorities."

The idea of affirmative action has always been conceptually difficult. It does not openly state that there has been overt discrimination in the past. It does not necessarily assume that racism or sexism has been operating. It is based on the painful phenomenon that blacks and women are grossly underrepresented in almost every occupation above those involving the least skilled persons. Affirmative action is designed to counter the negative action that brought about the exclusion of millions of persons because of their race or sex. Affirmative action does not say that unqualified persons must be hired but suggests that obviously many qualified persons have been excluded from positions because of a negative attitude toward them by those who do the hiring.

A dramatic example of affirmative action can be seen in the fact that President Carter in four years appointed more black lawyers to the federal bench than all other presidents taken together had ever done before. Why were not more black attorneys appointed to the federal bench prior to the Carter administration? That is the question that the administrators of affirmative action programs ask with respect to almost every category of workers in America.

Affirmative action programs operate with the hope that by education and example corporations and public agencies will voluntarily correct the racial and gender imbalances in their employment profile. But numerical and time goals are frequently necessary if an employer is to attain some substantial progress within a reasonable period. Hence, federal and state programs offer goals and timetables to employers and sometimes mandate them. Most employers are willing, even anxious, to have outside help to break the pattern of a predominantly white or male work force. Remarkable progress has been made in the roughly 15 years during which affirmative action has been the accepted practice of agencies that carry out the civil rights laws of the nation.

It is therefore baffling when the Justice Department insists that it is opposed in principle to affirmative action. It is, Mr. Reynolds insists, an attempt to cure discrimination by more discrimination. In its brief submitted in the Detroit case, the Justice Department stated that it "has profound doubts whether the Constitution permits governments to adopt remedies involving racial quotas to benefit persons who are not themselves the victims of discrimination — at least in the absence of a clear statement by Congress itself." This approach seeks to evade the fact of the massive underrepresentation of blacks in certain occupations by saying that "persons who are not themselves the victims of discrimination" have no claim on society. The idea of affirmative action was created precisely to reach those situations where overt racism did not necessarily exist but the results are the same as if it did exist. Affirmative action, in other words, is designed to reach the unconscious bias and the adherence to an unexamined custom that only whites should be waitresses or plumbers or police officers.

Mr. Reynolds further obscures what is actually the thinking of the Reagan administration when he insists that employment decisions should be color-blind. This approach, of course, would blot out many of the most helpful and healthy developments in the law of race relations over the past generation. Affirmative action assumes that public and private officials in the areas of education, housing and employment can and should be color sensitive. Mr. Reynolds seems so convinced that judgments arrived at with attention to color are undesirable that he has raised a serious question about the constitutionality of many color-conscious consent decrees entered into by the Justice Department in previous administrations.

In the three decisions in which the U.S. Supreme Court has ruled on affirmative action, it has not given support to the approach to affirmative action embraced by the Reagan administration. It has not, on the other hand, cleared up the conceptual or constitutional ambiguities inherent in the idea of hiring persons on criteria not exclusively related to their competence.

The five-to-four decision in 1978 requiring the University of California Medical School at Davis to admit Allan Bakke disallowed the relatively crude method of affirmative action employed by the admission officials at Davis. But the Bakke decision did not outlaw the use of race or minority status as one of the criteria for admission to a college. The court in fact went out of its way to praise the Harvard plan where race, along with other facts such as the ability to play the tuba, can be factored into the sophisticated formula employed for admissions. The majority decision in Bakke, moreover, approved of the use of race since it conceded that ethnic diversity is a legitimate and constitutionally acceptable goal of a university. Although the result and reasoning in Bakke are not free from ambiguity, that decision does not support the apparent position of the administration that affirmative action itself is neither required nor allowed.

The Supreme Court in 1979 in a six-to-three vote held that Brian F. Weber, a white employee of the Kaiser Aluminum & Chemical Corporation who had lost his place in a training program to a black, had no constitutional right to complain against the pact between labor and management which reserved half the openings in the training program for black employees. Mr. Reynolds denies that he ever said that the Weber decision was wrongly decided, but somehow he claims that the agreement to pursue affirmative action in the Weber situation would not be constitutional if it were pursued by public employers.

In 1980, the Supreme Court sustained a provision in a public works program enacted by Congress by which 10 percent of the work had to be granted (with some exceptions) to contracting companies controlled by minorities. The ruling in this case should probably be limited to the unique facts of this now discontinued federal program that was enacted, the Supreme Court noted, by a co-equal branch of government in order to deal with an acute crisis in the economy. But again there is no indication by the court that affirmative action or color-conscious programs are violations of the Constitution.

If the Supreme Court had decided to review the Detroit case and rule on the constitutionality of laying off white police officers with seniority over blacks in order to protect the objectives of affirmative action, it would have faced the toughest question yet. Federal Judge Damon J. Keith who presided at the Detroit trial held in a 73-page opinion that Detroit had for more than three decades used examinations and personnel tests that discriminated against black officers. Consequently, he ruled to sustain the affirmative action program even though this "upsets the expectations of white workers."

Blacks in Memphis won a similar victory where both the trial and appellate courts concluded that Memphis could not follow the "last-hired, first-fired" seniority rule because the objectives of affirmative action prevent the firing of recently hired blacks. This case has produced dozens of briefs by national organizations on both sides of the controversy. The A.F.L.-C.I.O. took the position of the Justice Department and urged that courts should not be allowed to displace "employees of one race who have done no wrong . . . to make room for persons of another race who have not been the victims of discrimination."

Up until the present time, it has been possible to continue to support the goals of affirmative action by holding that no whites will be hurt by it. Perhaps it will be possible to continue with that belief and conviction. An expanding economy makes it more possible to do so. But if jobs are phased out for any reason, hard choices between the rights of seniority and the rights obtained through affirmative action may have to be made. But to take an adamant position that all decisions made on affirmative action must yield to rights acquired by seniority is neither necessary nor required by the Constitution. Clearly, such a repudiation of affirmative action violates the spirit and even the letter of that vast body of law, custom and practice which has developed since 1965. That body of law was designed to change the America that the Kerner commission saw: two nations, "one white, one black."

The nation adopted affirmative action as an interim strategy for a period during which sex-based and race-rooted discrimination will gradually fade away. Affirmative action would not be needed if society could cure itself of treating women and blacks by stereotypes or by carefully concealed prejudices. Affirmative action is a technique designed to break the blindness of bias which has helped to produce a society with vast areas in which women and blacks are separated from the mainstream. To abolish affirmative action at this time is premature, unwise and destructive.

There are some legal and constitutional commentators who continue to raise hypotheticals about a possible Pandora's box if affirmative action is pressed too far. Not all of these critics of affirmative action were satisfied by the careful restraints imposed on affirmative action by the Bakke decision.

There are others who are opposed to affirmative action because they fear that a black or a woman will be placed ahead of them in the agency or corporation where they work. These fears are also present where there is a question of a minority challenge for places in schools or housing. But the remarkable thing about affirmative action is that it has worked as well as it has. Society has engaged in programs of affirmative action without requiring that everyone concede that the government and all of us owe restitution and reparation to black Americans because of what was done to them and to their ancestors for some 300 years. Affirmative action has remained fluid and flexible; it has requested voluntary compliance rather than requiring official submission. Affirmative action has so raised the consciousness of Americans that institutions are chagrined if their personnel are inordinately white or male. It seems unwise to press the Congress or the courts at this time for a definitive answer to the ultimate and enormously complicated questions involved in affirmative action. These questions are as difficult to articulate as to resolve. If white persons or males are being hurt — and there is little if any evidence of this — individual adjustments can be attempted. If unqualified blacks or women are being hired — and again the evidence is virtually nonexistent — training programs and modifications can be arranged.

Affirmative action recognizes that society must attempt to do something to correct the monumental mistakes made by generations of Americans toward blacks and women. Affirmative action calls for a sensitivity to the institutionalized prejudice whose existence cannot be denied. What this country did in tolerating slavery from 1619 to 1865 has distorted reality for millions of Americans. What it did by requiring segregated schools up to 1954 has further confused that reality. Affirmative action, however ambiguous and nebulous, is one answer to all of the many misconceptions that Americans have about blacks and women. Affirmative action should be clarified and refined, not scorned and abandoned.

Chapter 25

Is a Fair Housing Law a Forgotten Dream?

As the struggle to attain racially balanced schools and to make the working place multiracial continues, little is heard these days of the dream that always went with these two objectives — the creation of racially integrated neighborhoods. The Congress will have bills before it in 1984 to strengthen existing fair housing laws but any action in this area seems unlikely.

The Civil Rights Act of 1964 created the federal machinery to desegregate the schools by establishing a new civil rights office in the Department of Health, Education and Welfare Similarly, the civil rights law sought to integrate employment by the creation of the Equal Employment Opportunity Commission. Unfortunately, the far-reaching fair housing bill that passed the House in 1965 was sidetracked by a filibuster in the Senate. If a unit had been created within the Department of Housing and Urban Development to enforce a fair housing law, the shape of urban America might have been very different today. But the Fair Housing Law of 1968 was too weak to have the needed impact. A new and tough law is required. Indeed it may well be that the goals of racially mixed schools and an integrated work force may not be attainable until blacks and poor whites can acquire decent housing in the places they desire to live.

First published in *America*, April 7, 1984.

Government Complicity

The history of segregated schools and the massive exclusion of black workers from jobs is well known and is remembered with pain. But the same official policy kept blacks out of white neighborhoods until the 1960's. Federal policies, as spelled out in federal manuals, banned up until the 1960's the "infiltration of inharmonious racial or nationality groups" into all-white communities. Until at least 1948, federal housing policies contained an explicit endorsement of racism. Those policies eased a bit after the Supreme Court in 1948 forbade the enforcement of racially restrictive covenants. But until the 1960's the federal government never banned even one builder or developer from participating in Federal Housing Administration or Veterans Administration programs. The federal government never acted against real estate brokers who, by blockbusting and steering, helped to bring about the present patchwork of black and white neighborhoods.

In the presidential campaign of 1960, when federally subsidized discrimination in housing emerged as an issue, candidate John F. Kennedy stated that if elected he would sign an executive order to ban federally subsidized discrimination in housing with a "stroke of the pen." That order finally came — two years into the Kennedy Presidency. The order was narrowly construed so that it applied only to federally assisted housing contracted for after the date of the order. The federal agencies that supervised most of the mortgage lenders were excluded from the order at the last moment. The order covered less than 1 percent of the then existing inventory of housing and 15 percent of the new construction. The order had little impact on the patterns of segregated housing built up with the consent, if not the blessing, of the federal government over a period of several decades.

The existence of President Kennedy's executive order was used by the realtors and by others to keep housing out of the 1964 Civil Rights Act. As already noted, a fair housing measure failed in 1965.

In 1968, after the assassination of Martin Luther King Jr., Congress returned to its unfinished business in housing and enacted Title VIII, which contained a broad prohibition against discrimination in private and public housing. In June 1968 the Supreme Court in *Jones v. Mayer* ruled that the Reconstruction Civil Rights Act of 1866 was broad enough to provide black citizens with redress against private as well as governmental discrimination in housing transactions.

But the Fair Housing Act of 1968 was weaker than the measures Congress had provided for education, employment and voting. The housing bill failed to provide any adequate enforcement mechanism. H.U.D. could receive, investigate and conciliate complaints of housing discrimination, but it lacked the power to issue cease-and-desist orders or to order a remedy. The enforcement was also inadequate. Incredible as it sounds, no regulations were issued until 1972, and these were so inadequate that it must be said that the only meaningful regulations for the 1968 law were issued by the Carter administration in 1980 — only to be withdrawn in the early days of the Reagan administration.

Federal officials understood how intense the suburban resistance would be to the enforcement of a fair housing law. In 1971 President Nixon uttered these ambiguous and troubling words: "Whether rightly or wrongly, as they view the social conditions of urban slum life, many residents of the outlying areas are fearful that moving large numbers of persons — of whatever race — from the slums to their communities would bring a contagion of crime, violence, drugs and the other conditions from which so many of those who are trapped in the slums themselves want to escape."

In the years from 1969 through 1978 the Justice Department, using its power under the 1968 law to bring action against patterns of racial discrimination, initiated an average of 32 cases per year — striking at practices involving blockbusting, steering and discriminatory rental policies. The Justice Department sought to break patterns of segregation in housing and thereby to eliminate segregated schools.

In 1980 Congress returned to the inadequacies of the federal fair housing laws. A bill (H.R. 5200) sponsored by Congressman Don Edwards (D., Calif.) and me passed the House, but in December 1980 (after the election had changed the leadership of the Senate) it fell five votes short of the needed 60 to end a filibuster mounted by senators who opposed some of the reforms in the Edwards-Drinan bill and who wanted to require proof of intent rather than the current effects test.

The Reagan administration failed to propose any fair housing bill until late 1983, when the White House proposed a measure too weak even for acceptance by a coalition of Republicans anxious to eliminate the weaknesses in the 1968 Fair Housing Law.

Can a Fair Housing Bill Work?

The nation can look back at the past 20 years and claim with some pride that real advancements for minorities have been made in education, voting and employment. Indeed some of these advancements are almost spectacular, as for example, the dramatic banning of all those shameful forms of discrimination in voting that had permeated Southern elections for decades. A combination of a clear legal mandate and vigorous enforcement brought about a revolution in these areas.

Why has the progress been so slow in housing? The answer to that question sometimes seems more difficult as time goes on. The question of who is to live next door involves a deeper range of emotions than who is to be in one's child's classroom or who will work in the next office. Notions of private property and freedom of choice run deep when people contemplate any development that they fear might jeopardize the value of their homes or the privacy of their lives. As a candidate in 1976, Jimmy Carter reflected this fear when he said, "I have nothing against a community...trying to maintain the ethnic purity of their neighborhood." Candidate Carter later apologized for the use of the term "ethnic purity," but added that he would not "arbitrarily use federal force to change neighborhood patterns."

Other misunderstandings permeate the emotional issues of blacks moving into a predominantly white community. Will property value decrease? Will the area "tip" if one-fifth or one-fourth of the community becomes black? There is no evidence that these fears are any more difficult to deal with than comparable fears in the areas of education and employment. If the fair housing law that passed the House in 1965 had cleared the Senate and received the conscientious enforcement given to the Civil Rights Act of 1964 and the Voting Rights Act of 1965, would there now be many truly interracial communities throughout the country rather than the checkerboard pattern that exists almost everywhere? One cannot be entirely certain, but the answer is probably yes. In any event, the Congress cannot leave a major right like housing without strong federal protection and guarantees. It may be indeed that the failure to enact measures to guarantee open housing will in the end make integration in schools and jobs impossible to attain.

The availability of low-income housing is, of course, a central issue in the whole question of the enforcement of fair housing laws. If affordable housing is not available, the most sophisticated procedures to prevent discrimination against would-be minority purchasers are of no use. In 1982, H.U.D. estimated that more than 18 million families need housing assistance of some kind. With the slashes proposed by the administration in federal assistance to low-income people, that number may grow.

A presidential commission on housing reported in 1982 that the existing supply of housing is adequate but that the poor cannot afford to rent. That conclusion has been widely attacked by experts in the housing industry and by observers in the civil rights community. Civil rights specialists also see that low- and middle-income blacks are in effect prevented from acquiring property that they can afford because realtors engage in discriminatory practices knowing that the federal government will not prosecute.

An excellent treatment of many of these issues can be found in a 116-page study issued recently by former members of the U.S. Commission on Civil Rights now "in exile." Chaired by former Secretary of H.E.W. Arthur S. Flemming, the Citizens' Commission on Civil Rights documents how the Reagan administration made a weak fair housing law even weaker. The document shows in addition how the drastic cutback in subsidies for housing for the poor will make existing patterns of segregated housing even more difficult to rectify.

Shortly after the enactment of the weak fair housing bill in 1968, a national consensus emerged as to what the government should do to improve federal fair housing laws and their enforcement. There has been little dispute as to the elements needed for a strong fair housing law that will do for housing what federal laws have done for education, voting and employment. Those elements were contained in the bill that passed the House in 1980 but failed in the Senate.

Early in 1981 civil rights advocates tried to persuade the Reagan administration to go to Congress and obtain the enactment of that bill. The administration refused. After almost three years of delay the administration finally filed a bill that unfortunately had no constituency and that was virtually dead on arrival.

The fundamental measures that should be added to existing fair housing laws include the following:

1. Victims of housing discrimination should be able to secure relief without the necessity of filing a private lawsuit. This was provided for in H.R. 5200 by authorizing an administrative law judge within H.U.D. to sit in judgment on the allegation of the person denied a dwelling.

2. Injunctive relief should be provided to prevent the house or apartment being taken off the market before the complaint is adjudicated.

3. Protection should be extended to handicapped persons, to families with children and to single persons with or without children.

4. Reasonable attorney and expert witness fees should be available to the prevailing party.

5. Existing court decisions prohibiting racial redlining and discriminatory property insurance practices should be codified into statutory law.

Even if, however, all of these measures were enacted into law and enforced vigorously, discrimination in housing in many forms would probably continue. The practice of racial and ethnic groups being kept out of white communities is widespread and pervasive in the United States. It is one of the major reasons why busing is necessary to guarantee racially balanced schools. It is one of the principal reasons for interracial tensions and ethnic misunderstandings. It is certain that law alone cannot alter the way of life in cities where ethnic groups have lived in different areas for decades. But law can challenge and to some extent curb a practice that can have no foundation other than bigotry or at least ignorance. Law is a powerful force that teaches and gradually alters attitudes. Law has certainly had an amazing impact on the way Americans think about blacks in schools and factories. A fair housing law — enforced by continuous explanation, exhortation and counseling — would ease the anxieties and apprehensions of those who have never lived in any residential community that was not almost totally white. After these apprehensions have been softened, these individuals would be prepared to say that it is fundamentally unfair for white America to tell black people that they can have a right to have a job in a white factory and that their children can go to a predominantly white school, but that they themselves have no right to live in a neighborhood simply because no blacks have ever resided there.

Residential segregation is probably at the heart of every other form of segregation in the United States. It is harmful and costly. Unlike most major forms of racial discrimination, it is not forbidden by a law with strict civil and criminal penalties. The time has long since come for religious and civil rights groups to demand that segregated housing be dismantled and that racially integrated neighborhoods be created.

PART V

The Equal Rights
Amendment

Chapter 26

Equal Rights for Men and Women

Mr. Chairman, I rise to urge the adoption of House Joint Resolution 208 as originally introduced by my colleague from Michigan, Congresswoman Martha Griffiths, and to urge rejection of the version reported out by the full Judiciary Committee and of any other limitation upon the following clear, undiluted mandate:

> Equality of rights of any person under the law shall not be denied or abridged by the United States or by any State on account of sex.

I rise, therefore, to support effective constitutional recognition of the civil rights of women.

Both congressional and public debate on the equal rights amendment have been vigorous and thorough. In March and April, subcommittee no. 4 of the Judiciary Committee heard the testimony of dozens of distinguished citizens — lawyers and laymen, students, religious and professional leaders, representatives from business and labor — a diversity of interests reflecting the momentousness of what we consider today. The policy embodied in the Equal Rights Amendment rises to a level of profound social importance which fully justifies its incorporation in the Constitution.

My own position is succinctly expressed in the separate views of the Judiciary Committee's report on House Resolution 208, in which I join 13 of my colleagues in concluding that —

First published in the *Congressional Record*, October 12, 1971.

> "Equality" is perhaps the one word which more than any other challenges our government to fulfill its constitutional commitments to all of our people.... Until now the concept of a qualified form of equality — of an equality that can be abridged so long as a suitable rationalization can be found — has been repugnant to our Constitution.

Of all the appeals to their country's conscience being issued by American women, perhaps the most powerful is that women must have equal rights in employment. Extraordinary consequences flow from the role of work in our society. When one American asks another "What do you do?" —and this is often the first question between strangers — what he really means is "Who are you?" Too frequently, women must answer this question with embarrassment and dissatisfaction. In the area of employment, men and women are simply not equal under the law.

On the state level, sex discrimination in employment is pervasive. On the one hand, there is the active injustice of the mislabeled "protective legislation." A pointed refutation of any need for these laws is the statement, on August 19, 1969, of the Equal Employment Opportunity Commission:

> The Commission believes that such state laws and regulations, although originally promulgated for the purpose of protecting females, have ceased to be relevant to our technology or to the expanding role of the female worker in our economy. The Commission has found that such laws and regulations do not take into account the capacities, preferences, and abilities of individual females and tend to discriminate rather than protect...

Three weeks ago, the House by a narrow margin rejected legislation that would have given the Commission effective "cease and desist power" to begin to cure these inequities.

In the face of continuing sex discrimination by private employers, state administrations remain generally inert. In more than half of the states, no laws prohibit employers from discriminating against women in hiring or firing, in fringe benefits, in wages and promotion, in training programs, or in the setting of job categories, and the placing of classified advertisements.

The combination of state discriminatory practice and state default in the presence of discrimination frequently excludes women from employment altogether. It has routinely restricted their job opportunity — their freedom to choose suitable, fulfilling work and to advance in it. Depressing statistics which reflect this situation are only too readily available:

In 1968 the average woman college graduate was earning $6,694 a year, while the average man with an 8th grade education was earning almost as much, $6,580.

In 1969, 51 percent of women who actually worked at fulltime jobs were earning less than $5,000 a year, while less than 17 percent of the male work force was earning that little.

The median wage of women in relation to men has been decreasing from 64 percent in 1955, to 61 percent in 1960, to 58 percent in 1969.

The unemployment rate for women is higher than for men: in April 1970, it was 5.7 percent for women against 4.2 percent for men.

Any language which would qualify the constitutional requirement of equality in the discredited name of "protection" would only entrench such inequities. That they, in fact, require a constitutional reply is the bitter lesson of the history of inaction of state legislatures and of the Supreme Court under the 14th Amendment, a history thoroughly documented in a comprehensive analysis published in the April 1971 issue of the *Yale Law Review*. The authors of that article, including Yale's distinguished constitutional scholar Thomas I. Emerson, demonstrate that the Supreme Court has never found a sex-based qualification to violate the equal protection clause and that piecemeal legislative reform "at least by itself simply lacks the breadth, coherence, and economy of political effort necessary for fundamental change in the legal position of women."

Without a constitutional amendment the burden of change will remain essentially with the advocates of equal rights. With the amendment, the burden will for the first time be shifted to where it should always have lain, with any who seek to erect new barriers to equality or to preserve the vestiges of old ones.

I certainly do not share the fear expressed by some opponents of an unqualified equal rights amendment that its enactment would produce "judicial chaos." The disappearance of an unjust but familiar orderliness will always seem chaotic to some. Indeed, in many respects, this is precisely the type of situation — the need to elaborate and rationalize the consequences of a fundamental legislative change — where the judicial process is most relevant and effective.

While I do not underestimate the possible problems in implementing the Equal Rights Amendment, I would point out that the central legal principles involved are ones with which our courts have had long experience under the 14th Amendment. As the *Yale Law Review* article asserts:

> The fundamental legal principle underlying the Equal Rights Amendment, then, is that the law must deal with particular attributes of individuals not with a classification based on the broad and impermissible attribute of sex. This principle, however, does not preclude legislation (or other official action), which regulates, takes into account, or otherwise deals with a physical characteristic unique to one sex.

Legislation of this type would resolve many of the situations which opponents of the Equal Rights Amendment have cited as sources of judicial "chaos" if the amendment were enacted. For example, a law establishing medical leave for childbearing would be permissible, because it applies to a physical characteristic unique to women. A law establishing leave for women only, for child rearing, would not be permissible.

Another area where "chaos" has been unjustifiably prophesied centers around the separation of sleeping quarters and rest rooms in public institutions and facilities. As the authors of the *Yale Law Review* article state:

> The great concern over these matters expressed by opponents of the Equal Rights Amendment seems not only to have been magnified beyond all proportion but to have failed to take into account the impact of the young, but fully recognized constitutional right of privacy.

The courts will be required to balance the two conflicting rights: the right not to be discriminated against on the basis of sex with, on the other hand, the right to privacy. The right of privacy would justify the separation of the sexes in public rest rooms, in the sleeping quarters of prisons, and within the armed forces.

Aside from the relatively immediate and visible consequences of enactment of this amendment — judicial reexamination of the state "protective work laws," for example — there will undoubtedly arise indirect but profound effects on the processes of our daily lives. Many of these effects we cannot now foresee. Surely, however, we should have nothing to fear from the constitutional recognition of the civil rights of American women. The law is a model and the Equal Rights Amendment can only be a model that will dignify the relationships between men and women.

I believe the House will honor itself today by approving the Equal Rights Amendment without reservation or qualification.

Chapter 27

The Role of Women in the 1980's

The expectations which society has for women have changed more in the past 20 years than in the previous 20 centuries. Women are expected to be professionals, wives, mothers and leaders of public opinion. And the revolution in the expectations which humanity has for women have not yet finished.

We rejoice in the progress made as, for instance, in the fact that the number of women in law and medical schools is approaching 50%. But we lament the shocking under-representation of women in many places, for example, in the Congress where there are less than 20 women out of 535 members.

Wellesley College was one of the major architects many decades ago of that revolution which we see unfolding today. This distinguished and venerable institution believed from the beginning in the rights of women and the exalted role which they should have in the life of humanity.

In the 1980's the graduates of Wellesley College will have to face more complex challenges than any previous generation of women. They will face unsettling questions which will have to be settled, baffling dilemmas which have to be resolved and personal choices which cannot be postponed. Underlying all of these problems will be the still evolving idea which the world will have of the role and destiny of women in modern society. That role and destiny is being touched upon at least in a confused way in the debate over the Equal Rights Amendment. If three more states ratify the ERA and it becomes a part of the

Baccalaureate Address, Wellesley College, 1981.

United States Constitution, new and broader horizons will open up for women. If, on the other hand, the ERA is not ratified, there may be a turning back in the advances which we have experienced regarding the place of women in society. But any such reaction would be only temporary because the revolution for the rights of women and for an equal place in society for women has been won. But as in all post-revolutionary eras, there are implications to be thought through.

Let me discuss the new role of women with regard to the arms race and global hunger.

Can we blame the military madness of the world on men? Men are its architects. They spend $525 billion per year on arms — well over $1 billion every single day. They have accumulated 50,000 nuclear weapons, 30,000 of which are in the possession of the United States. They have over 30 million men under arms.

Have men locked women out of all of this madness? The answer is yes. Would the situation be less ominous if the generals and the soldiers were 50% women? We cannot guarantee it, but things could hardly be worse.

Is there some "macho" instinct in men which makes them aspire to war? We cannot be certain, but men, not women, have been making war for centuries.

Should women aspire to have control equal to men over the military? The answer has to be yes. Right now women have virtually nothing to say about the expenditures this year of $152 billion by the Pentagon. Will women have anything to say during the next five years when that sum will climb to the unbelievable amount of $343 billion to be spent each year by the Pentagon? Not unless women rise up in a revolt against their almost total exclusion from the military decision-making process in the federal government.

Women are beginning to get equal status at the bar, in the executive suites, on medical staffs of hospitals and even in some churches. But they are almost non-existent at the Pentagon.

It is distressing that one does not even hear pleas — even from women — that this situation be corrected. Do people — even women — think that war and preparations for war belong exclusively to men? If women participated in the formulation of American military policy, I have to believe that it would be less hideous than it is now.

Closely related to the male-dominated military policy of this country and the world, is the agony over global hunger. One-sixth of humanity — 800 million persons — are chronically malnourished. At least 20 million persons die each year from starvation. Of the 80 million infants that will be born in the Third World in 1981, 25 million will die before they are five years old.

Again, women have little to do with the decision process that allows this scandal to continue. Would the disasters be fewer if half of the decision-makers with respect to aid to the under-developed nations were made by women? I think so. Women could not have tolerated 350 million children having no school to go to in the international year of the child. Women would do more to prevent any increase in the number of children blind from malnutrition — now 42 million in the Third World. Women certainly would not have allowed the United States to be the one nation in the world to vote to allow mothers in the Third World to be misled about infant feeding formulas.

Dramatic break-throughs for women are imminent. The centuries during which humanity systematically denied equal-ity to women are over. Society is filled with guilt over its incredible war against women. Like the sinner seeking reconci-liation, man today wants to honor women by giving them equal pay, equal opportunity and equal respect.

You will be the beneficiaries of this new enlightenment. Your lives will be significantly richer than those of your moth-ers. You will have opportunities never given to women in all of human history.

Will you utilize these unprecedented opportunities to their fullest extent? Or will history record that the first generation of American women able to serve as Secretary of Defense, Justices of the United States Supreme Court, Chief Executive Officer of General Motors, and President of Harvard Univer-sity were disappointing? History will record that if women, when they come into moral and political power never available to them before, failed to slow the arms race and do little to alleviate global hunger. These are the twin problems which will not wait much longer for solutions. If they become aggravated or if they cause wars and revolutions around the globe — as well they might — history will be able, rightly or wrongly, to blame women if, for the first time in the history of the world, one half of the key decision-makers in America are women.

The lesson is clear. Young women who receive the finest education available in America should study and understand the anguish of the arms race and the agony of global hunger so that they will be in a position to help to resolve them.

It seems self evident that women now in their 20's will have more opportunities thrust upon them than any previous group of women in American history. Not a few will say that women are moving up too rapidly. Some will even organize to drive women back to the home. And, undoubtedly, there will be more Phyllis Shafley's who will long for the days when women were the weaker sex, dependent on men for their support and for their status.

A bold new day is here for women. As never before in the history of the world, they will be able to control their lives. Some young women will undoubtedly be afraid of the unchartered pilgrimage which they will be expected to undertake. Others will lead lives filled with confusion because of unresolved conflicts over the priorities to be given to family, children and careers. Others, perhaps most, will be looking to traditional moral values as compasses for a voyage that has never before been sailed by any women in any previous generation.

Wellesley College began educating women for these challenges generations ago. The founders knew that for centuries women had been repressed and humiliated. With admirable foresight the founders of Wellesley College structured an institution designed to prepare women to be educators, statespersons and leaders. Today that institution gives you its prestigious degree and prayerfully sends you into a world where, finally, after centuries of humiliation, women will be accepted as equal partners with men in the development of a global village in which economic justice and political tranquility can hopefully be combined to bring about a millennium of peace.

Chapter 28

ERA Defeat Poses New Problem

I will be sad and depressed on June 30, 1982, if the Equal Rights Amendment fails to become the 27th amendment to the Constitution.

I recall well the day it cleared the House Judiciary Committee in 1971. The House then voted for it 354 to 34; the Senate approved it 84 to 8. Twenty-two states ratified it in the first nine months after its passage. The trouble began in the mid-1970s.

The arguments against the ERA seemed preposterous. Its opponents alleged that the ERA would require uni-sex toilets, extend the draft to women and weaken the rights of divorcing women. But apparently these arguments were believable and were even believed. At first there was some feeling that these contentions were the product of a tiny group of near hysterical rightwing extremists whose appeal would quickly fade.

But as the original seven-year deadline for ratification of March 22, 1979, approached, the National Organization of Women and many other groups asked the House Judiciary Committee to extend the deadline for another seven years. The opponents of ERA claimed this was "changing the rules in the middle of the game." After mighty battles the Congress, by a majority vote (not by two-thirds), extended the period of ratification for 30 months.

ERA proponents have been disappointed by the lack of leadership on this issue by the Catholic bishops of the United States. I have heard the complaint not infrequently that the

First published in the *National Catholic Reporter*, June 18, 1982.

bishops are very articulate and aggressive in enunciating their view on Central America, abortion, nuclear weapons, tax credits for parents with children in private schools and cutbacks in federal funds for social programs. Why then have the Catholic bishops been silent on the ERA? In the post-mortems on ERA after June 30, 1982, there will be plenty of blame to go around, and the Catholic bishops will be given a share.

Bishop Michael McAuliffe of Jefferson City, Missouri, chairman of the Bishops Committee on Rights and Responsibilities, did his best to have his belief in the ERA accepted by his fellow bishops. He testified on behalf of the ERA before the Missouri Senate. Similarly, Bishop Walter Sullivan of Richmond, Virginia, spoke out for the ERA in January 1982, as did Bishop Maurice J. Dingman of Des Moines in October 1980. Recently Bishop Raymond Lucker of New Ulm, Minnesota, did the same. Until this month, only two other bishops were known to have spoken out in favor of ERA — Bishop George Evans of Denver and now-retired Bishop Charles Buswell of Pueblo, Colorado. Then this month 23 bishops issued a joint statement asking for ERA ratification.

In 1977 the National Conference of Catholic Charities passed a resolution endorsing the ERA, as did the Canon Law Society in 1979 and the Conference of Major Superiors of Men.

For reasons which frankly I do not understand, the bishops did not approve the ratification of what is without doubt the most important moral and legal aspiration of American women in the last 50 years.

The silence of the Catholic bishops left them out of the mainstream of religious thought on the ERA. Among groups that endorse the ERA are the National Council of Churches, the United Church of Christ and the nation's major organizations of Jews, Baptists, Methodists, Lutherans, Presbyterians and Quakers.

Were the Catholic bishops influenced by the charge of some opponents of the ERA that the passage of this amendment would somehow further legalize abortion? The Leadership Conference of Women Religious rejected that contention and stated that "the issues around which the abortion debate rages are not the issues entailed in the ERA ... persons who are strongly anti-abortion can be, with full moral integrity, just as strongly pro-ERA."

A definitive article in *America* magazine April 12, 1980, by Sister Maureen Fiedler and Elizabeth Alexander documented the evidence for that conclusion.

No one can say that the bishops' approval could have changed the views of those legislators who oppose the ERA, some of whom apparently believe with the Reverend Jerry Falwell that God desired the defeat of the ERA. Nor could the bishops have altered the views of the Mormon-dominated states, all of which turned down the ERA. But could an official Catholic position favoring the ERA have turned the tide in Illinois, Missouri and Louisiana — all three of which have rejected the ERA?

The death of the ERA has without doubt monumental consequences for the church, for women and for the law. The church will be seen by some as guilty of sexism. Others may charge the church with being misinformed, intimidated, misled, mistaken, or all of the above.

For women, the defeat of the ERA has to be categorized as a disaster. The people of the United States have unbelievably refused to place in their Constitution a 27th amendment which contains the following elementary standard of basic equality: "Equality of rights under the law shall not be denied or abridged by the United States or by any state on account of sex."

Psychologically and emotionally the repudiation, the rejection and the rebuff are painful and humiliating for women and, let us hope, for men.

The demise of the ERA poses difficult questions for the law. Will the claim by women for certain rights based on equality now be rejected in the absence of a specific statute? Does the defeat of the ERA mean that the 14th Amendment, which does not mention sex, should now be construed not to include equality based on gender because an amendment outlawing discrimination based on sex was rejected by the people?

Other equally painful questions must be asked by courts and by legislatures. Their answers almost certainly will narrow rather than expand opportunities for women.

What should the proponents of the ERA do now? Start the process again in Congress seeking ratification? Request another extension of the time during which the three necessary states might ratify? Go the way of statutes and forbid at the federal and state level all forms of discrimination based on sex?

Each of these alternatives contains problems which are more agonizing than one wants to contemplate at this moment. But one or more of them must be accepted and advocated. One road to obtain true equality for women in the United States has disappeared. Another road must surely be found.

Is it too much to hope that a newly energized Catholic hierarchy might this time be in the forefront of the campaign to place into U.S. law a guarantee that the women of the United States can never be discriminated against because of their sex?

PART VI

The Death Penalty

Chapter 29

Abolish the Death Penalty

Mr. Speaker, today with 26 of my colleagues I am introducing legislation to abolish the death penalty under all federal laws.

The timing of this legislation could hardly be more appropriate. For today President Nixon has transmitted to Congress a state of the union message on criminal justice that calls upon Congress to reinstate the death penalty in certain circumstances as a means of combating serious crime.

Only last June the Supreme Court held, in *Furman* v. *Georgia* (408 U.S. 238), that infliction of capital punishment is unconstitutional under the cruel and unusual punishment clause of the 8th Amendment. While many, including myself, read the Court's decision as prohibiting the death penalty under all circumstances, others, including President Nixon, interpret the decision as leaving a narrow zone of situations in which capital punishment may be constitutionally inflicted.

In view of the controversy surrounding the Court's decision, and particularly in light of the president's proposals, I am persuaded that this issue should be finally resolved by Congress.

I would like to quote from Mr. Justice Blackmun's dissenting opinion in *Furman v. Georgia:*

> I yield to no one in depth of my distaste, antipathy, and, indeed, abhorrence for the death penalty, with all its aspects of physical distress and fear and of moral judgment exercised

First published in the *Congressional Record*, March 14, 1973.

by finite minds. That distaste is buttressed by a belief that capital punishment serves no useful purpose that can be demonstrated. For me, it violates childhood's training and life's experiences and it is not compatible with the philosophical convictions I have been able to develop. It is antagonistic to any sense of "reverence for life." *Were I a legislator, I would vote against the death penalty for the policy reasons argued by counsel for the respective petitioners and expressed and adopted in the several opinions filed by the Justices who vote to reverse these convictions.* [Emphasis supplied.]

Like Mr. Justice Blackmun, I see the necessity for Congress' immediate action in this matter. In introducing this legislation I would like to comment upon the president's proposed reinstatement of the death penalty and then review the arguments for and against capital punishment.

The president bases his support for renewed capital punishment on a simplistic "big stick" theory of justice. So as to attempt to evade the Supreme Court's aversion to the arbitrary nature of past administration of the death penalty, the president's proposal suggests a scheme that would allow the death penalty to be imposed for the crimes of "war-related treason," "sabotage," and most significantly, "all specifically enumerated crimes under Federal jurisdiction from which death results."

This last category is tantamount to opening the floodgates of government-licensed executions. It is indicative of the president's shortsighted view that justice is a matter of "eye-for-an-eye" vengeance — not correction.

The president would attempt to avoid the constitutional limitations on the death penalty by authorizing the sentencing judge or jury to automatically impose the death penalty "where it is warranted." After the trial and prior to sentencing, a hearing would be held to consider either aggravating or mitigating factors in the case. If one mitigating factor is found, then the death penalty could not be imposed. In the absence of mitigating factors and in the presence of aggravating factors, imposition of the death penalty would be mandatory.

The fallacy of the president's plan is that there is no evidence whatever that the reinstatement of capital punishment will have the effect of reducing the number of serious and violent crimes. The traditional reluctance of juries to send a man to his death can hardly be expected to vanish overnight. The situation will in all likelihood develop where juries continually find mitigating circumstances so as to avoid the mandatory imposition of a penalty which, as is obvious to all, cannot be reversed once executed.

Aside from the fact that this scheme does not remove the possibility than an innocent man may be sent to his death, it is highly doubtful whether this still arbitrary and cruel penalty would survive constitutional scrutiny by the courts. And apart from this consideration, there is no evidence other than the rhetoric of the president and his followers to support the claim that the reinstatement of the death penalty will in fact cut down on the number of crimes. Quite to the contrary, the overwhelming bulk of evidence — supported not by unrealistic social theorists as the president infers, but by eminent jurists and dedicated students of justice, as well as the undeservedly maligned social theorists — suggests that the use of the death penalty has virtually no effect in deterring serious and violent crimes.

The president's criminal justice philosophy — if it can be called that — appeals to the worst and most irrational instincts of fallible man. Even a man presumably of the president's own political persuasions, Mr. Justice Blackmun, whom the president appointed to the Supreme Court, decries the inhumanity and ineffectiveness of capital punishment. The president's National Commission on Reform of Federal Criminal Laws recommended to him in 1971 that capital punishment be abolished. But the president has spurned these learned opinions, and has sought to solve the pressing problem of crime not through positive, realizeable measures which attack the roots of crime, but through dramatic, harsh punitive measures.

"Law and order" slogans and rhetorical fearmongering will not solve the problem of crime, and neither will temporary reinstatement of the dying concept of judicial murder. Capital punishment is more of an indictment of a society than a benefit to it. It is inhumane.

An important study of the deterrent impact of the death

penalty was made by Thorsten Sellin in a report for the model
penal code project of the American Law Institute. Studies of
the homicide rates in contiguous jurisdictions with and without
the death penalty show that states with and without the death
penalty had virtually identical murder rates and trends. There
was no correlation between the status of the death penalty and
the homicide rate, according to the study. It was also found that
there was no significant decrease or increase in the murder rate
following an execution, and that police and prison homicides
are virtually the same in abolition states as in death penalty
states. Sellin concluded:

> Anyone who carefully examines the...data is bound to
> arrive at the conclusion that the death penalty, as we use it,
> exercises no influence on the extent or fluctuating rates of
> capital crime. It has failed as a deterrent.

The way in which the death penalty is administered also
undermines its effectiveness as a deterrent. In order to be
effective, punishment must be administered immediately, consistently, and relentlessly, and the public must expect this to
happen in all cases. The actual practice of capital punishment
does not satisfy any of these conditions. Historically, only a
small proportion of first-degree murderers were sentenced to
death and even fewer were executed. The delay in the conviction and execution of capital offenders is common. This would
hardly enable someone contemplating a horrible crime to visu-
alize the death penalty. According to a study by the American
Bar Foundation, another effect of long delays in capital trials
and executions is a weakening of public confidence in the law.

One of the chief purposes of capital punishment has been the
absolute restraint of the offender. Supporters of the death
penalty argue that this is the only way to protect society against
further crimes by convicted murderers. But is such an extreme
measure really necessary, when the alternative, life imprisonment, is an adequate protective measure? Evidence has shown
that murderers generally make the best prisoners and have one
of the lowest recidivism rates. The vision of a paroled murderer
as danger to the public has been exaggerated. Statistics have
pointed out that the behavior of a first-degree murderer

released on parole is very good — better even than those paroled from lesser crimes such as property offenders. I do not mean to suggest that parole for a convicted murderer is or should be easily obtained. A study of "incorrigibles" to prevent others from similar behavior would certainly benefit society more than the execution of these individuals, as would reform of parole and pardon practices and prison conditions.

One of the important arguments against the institution of capital punishment is that it is irrevocable. Unlike any other form of punishment, it forever deprives an individual of the benefit of new law or of new evidence that might affect his conviction. The passage of time, further investigations, and studies of specific cases have shown that innocent men have been wrongly accused and convicted of first-degree murder in the United States. Execution of the innocent raises an important and serious question about the validity of the death penalty.

There is no question in my mind that human life is a highly cherished value that should give way only upon a persuasive showing that capital punishment serves a prime social purpose that cannot otherwise be served. This has not been shown. One of the reasons we must value human life so highly is that human beings are capable of rationality and moral conviction. Do we wish to create an atmosphere of violence by advocating capital punishment as a form of vengeance? The idea of an individual in a courtroom fighting for his life is hardly compatible with the idea of justice and fairness as the goals of our legal system. The purpose of criminal law is and should be to provide protection against volence. But in invoking the death penalty, we are motivated by the same irrationality as the criminal who acted violently. This hardly justifies the death penalty.

At best, the death penalty is applied randomly; at worst it is applied discriminatorily. It is rigged against the poor, the friendless, and members of minority groups. As such, it violates the constitutional guarantee of equality before the law. By remaining sporadic and random, capital punishment has no status as a regular and rational part of criminal justice. The selection of juries and officials creates rampant opportunities for class and racial discrimination. Of 455 men executed for rape in this country since 1930, 90 percent were black. Of those who were executed for murder since 1930, 49 percent were black. In an overwhelming number of cases, it was people who were unable to afford expert and dedicated legal counsel who received the penalty of death.

The trend of history is overwhelmingly toward the abolition of capital punishment. Once in use everywhere for a great variety of crimes, the death penalty has been virtually abandoned in practice. The move toward disuse of the death penalty in America has been paralleled and largely outstripped by the rest of the world. In Europe, only France and Spain have retained the death penalty. In South America it survives only in a few of the smaller countries and in three out of the 33 Mexican jurisdictions. Canada has suspended the death penalty for a period of 5 years. A recent report by the Secretary General of the United Nations concludes that:

> Those countries retaining the death penalty report that in practice it is only exceptionally applied and frequently the persons condemned are later pardoned by executive authority.

As the world's leading legal killer, the Republic of South Africa executes about 100 men per year — most of them black. Do we wish to top this and execute all 582 men on our death rows?

In the United States, 39 states still authorize capital punishment, but the discretionary features of sentencing make contemporary use of the death penalty far less frequent than its authorizations on the statute books might suggest. Capital punishment occurs only in a fraction of cases where it can be legally imposed, a fraction which has been steadily decreasing since 1935. Since 1967, there have been no executions at all in this country.

Let me sum up the reasons for the abolishment of the death penalty: In my view the taking of a human life is morally unacceptable; capital punishment does not serve as a corrective measure because it does not provide for the rehabilitation of criminals; capital punishment is not a deterrent to crimes and is ineffective, because of long delays of sentencing and execution;

capital punishment is a violation of due process because there are no standards to guide the judge or the jury in the exercise of it, and it allows discrimination by race and class; capital punishment violates the mark of a civilized society because it contradicts the ideal of human dignity; capital punishment is a cruel and excessive and irrevocable punishment, which serves society less adequately than life imprisonment.

President Nixon now has the burden of proving his case for capital punishment against the great weight of research in the social sciences and against the even heavier burden of the Nation's conscience. I am confident that in the end reason will prevail. It is now up to Congress to ensure the abolition of capital punishment once and for all.

Chapter 30

One Step Closer to Execution

In two decisions July 6, the U.S. Supreme Court made it clear that a majority of at least five of the justices are not about to change their position that the states may constitutionally demand the death penalty. Justice Thurgood Marshall, in vigorous dissent, continued his long-held position that capital punishment violates the mandate in the 8th Amendment against "cruel and unusual" punishment. Justices Harry A. Blackmun and William J. Brennan, also in dissent, advanced other reasons why the death penalty, at least as applied, cannot stand constitutional muster.

But the two 6-3 decisions seemed to mark the end of a long line of at least a dozen opinions since 1972 in which the Supreme Court has made it clear that it will not ban the taking of the life of a person who has committed murder.

The July 6 decisions were in sharp contrast with the 361-245 vote of the English House of Commons July 12, affirming the decision made by Great Britain in 1965 to abolish capital punishment.

No one can be certain whether executions will now come rapidly for the 1,200 persons on death row. But after the July 6 decision in the case of Thomas Barefoot, the psychiatrists of America are now involved as never before in the issue of capital punishment. In 1978 Barefoot was convicted of the murder of a police officer in Texas. Under state law the prosecution was required to prove beyond every reasonable doubt that "there is

First published in the *National Catholic Reporter*, September 2, 1983.

a probability that the defendant would commit criminal acts of violence that would constitute a continuing threat to society."

Pursuant to this requirement the state called two psychiatrists who, in response to hypothetical questions, testified that Barefoot would in their judgment be dangerous in the future. The jury believed the psychiatrists and recommended the death penalty. On appeal the defense urged that the use of psychiatrists to make predictions about the accused's future conduct was unconstitutional, because psychiatrists individually and as a class are not competent to predict future dangerousness.

The evidence for their contention is impressive. The American Psychiatric Association (APA) has demonstrated that psychiatric testimony about a defendant's future dangerousness is wrong two times out of three. Indeed the APA, in its friend of the court brief in the Barefoot case, expressed its firm institutional policy that psychiatrists have no expertise in predicting long-term future dangerousness. Psychiatrists as a matter of fact consistently err on the side of overpredicting violence.

The recommendation of the death penalty for Barefoot, induced to a significant if not an overwhelming degree by the testimony of two psychiatrists, is offensive to the APA standards for another reason. These norms declare that "it it unethical for a psychiatrist to offer a professional opinion unless he/she has conducted an examination." The vehement dissent of Blackmun points out that the Supreme Court, in affirming Barefoot's conviction, "sanctions the admission . . . of medical testimony so unreliable and unprofessional that it violates the canons of medical ethics."

In the second July 6 decision, the Supreme Court affirmed the conviction of Elwood Barclay for murder in Florida. The majority ruling made it clear once again the Supreme Court is unlikely to shift its basic position that the states may execute so long as they follow the procedural safeguards set forth by the Supreme Court.

One ray of possible hope for those opposed to the death penalty came when the Supreme Court, in June 1983, set aside the conviction of a man sentenced to life without parole under the habitual offender law of North Dakota. In an unprecedented decision the majority of the court said life imprisonment for a series of crimes not involving serious felonies violates the constitutional prohibition against "cruel and unusual" punishment. Could this reasoning apply to the death penalty? Not in the minds of the majority of the Burger court.

With the rejection of hanging by England the United States finds itself even more isolated from the rest of the world with respect to executing murderers. No democratic country in Europe now uses the death penalty. In Latin America it is practically unknown. There was only one hanging in Japan last year. Western Australia will abolish the death penalty next year.

The countries that still execute people include South Africa, where capital punishment is employed for robbery and rape as well as murder. An average of 100 people are hanged each year in South Africa, one of them white. In the Soviet Union 23 crimes are punishable by death, including selling for profit; although statistics are not reliable, it is estimated some 400 criminals are shot each year.

At Fort Leavenworth, Kansas, U.S. military officials detain seven men on death row. The armed forces have not executed a soldier since 1961. The death penalty was not apparently indispensable during the war in Vietnam. Congress has been unwilling to update federal law to permit the execution of soldiers found guilty of a capital crime. The only federal law that now permits the death penalty to be applied pursuant to the procedural safeguards required by the Supreme Court involves the hijacking of an airplane.

In 1984 will the United States execute more people than South Africa and the Soviet Union? The scene is now set for such an eventuality. Perhaps the only consolation will be that Iran, according to Amnesty International, executed 5,195 people from February 1979 to June 1983.

Chapter 31

Can Churches Curb Death Penalty?

What will church groups do for the 1,166 men and 12 women who are death row inmates scheduled for execution during the next few months?

In mid-January 1983, Pope John Paul II became the first pontiff in history to urge abolition of the death penalty. Speaking to the Vatican Diplomatic Corps, the pope called on the world's governments to grant clemency or to pardon prisoners sentenced to death.

The U.S. bishops condemned the death penalty before the recent plea by the Holy Father. Capital punishment has been abolished in most Catholic countries, including Italy. France threw out the guillotine in late 1981.

But church groups' opposition to the death penalty does not seem to be influencing Americans. The Harris Poll recently recorded that while only 38 per cent of all Americans approved of capital punishment in 1965, that figure rose to 68 per cent in 1983.

In Massachusetts in November 1982, a state more than 60 per cent Catholic, the voters elected to reinstate capital punishment even though the Catholic bishops of the Bay State spoke out strongly against the death penalty. All but 12 states now authorize it.

The only significant victory for those who would abolish capital punishment was the March 10 veto by New York Governor Mario Cuomo of a measure designed to broaden

First published in the *National Catholic Reporter*, May 27, 1983.

New York's law which now covers only prison inmates who kill a corrections employee.

The United States Supreme Court is trying to resolve a dispute as to whether a federal appeals court must grant a stay of execution to condemned convicts who have filed for habeas corpus, but who are not yet able to show they are raising a substantial new issue. If the nation's highest tribunal rules negatively, the nation could see three executions a week starting in late 1983.

Lawyers involved in the appeals of those on death row — and especially attorneys with the NAACP Legal Defense Fund — have demonstrated that one-third to one-half of all on death row would have their convictions reversed if they can obtain adequate and experienced counsel. That means some 400 of the 1,178 persons now on death row would not die if they had a competent attorney able to review all potential reversible errors in their trials!

Several facts about the current, unprecedented situation are disturbing:

1. Forty-two per cent of the condemned prisoners are black, although only 11 per cent of the total population in the United States is black.

2. Of the 1,178 persons condemned, 470 are in three states — Florida (195), Texas (151) and California (124).

3. Those states where the death penalty is not authorized — such as Michigan, Minnesota, Rhode Island and Wisconsin — do not have more murders than states where the death penalty is allowed.

Every night when the United States Supreme Court has to make a decision on another appeal of a person about to be executed, Amnesty International conducts a quiet vigil across the street from the Supreme Court building. Seven executions have occurred since the death penalty was reinstated in 1976.

I have been present at the Amnesty International vigil on several evenings when the last appeals on these seven and other cases were being acted on by the Supreme Court. No one feels comfortable about the process. Why should five out of nine judges be able or required to decide in haste at the 11th hour about the death that evening of a person on death row?

Justice Lewis Powell recently spoke out about this awkward situation and urged that the death penalty be suspended unless Congress and the courts come forward with a process of appeal which is fair and perceived to be fair. It may be that such a process cannot be devised until the fundamental difficulty in the death penalty process is resolved — that the sentence of death is decreed disproportionately on blacks, the uneducated and the poor.

Most advanced nations have given up capital punishment because humanity has come to the conclusion that the guillotine, the gallows and the electric chair are gruesome. Within the past year four states —Arkansas, Massachusetts, Montana and Washington — have provided for death by lethal injection as an alternative to other forms of execution. But is this only cosmetic?

It does not seem to reach the essential issue: does the death penalty deter murder? There is no conclusive evidence on that point. Consequently, can the state require the supreme penalty of criminals when it is not clear or certain that the exaction of such an extreme measure is needed for society's safety or security?

The wisdom and fairness of the death penalty are ancient issues on which emotions and prejudices are deeply felt. Political leaders are not likely to urge repeal of the death penalty now that an unprecedented 68 per cent of the American people favor it. Senator Strom Thurmond (R-S.C.), chairman of the Senate Judiciary Committee, wants to expand the one federal capital offense — airplane hijacking — to several others. President Reagan proposed a broad federal death penalty in legislation he filed in March 1983.

Considering the political climate, only a broad-based citizens' movement is likely to influence the current atmosphere which is so much in favor of capital punishment. Amnesty International, the American Civil Liberties Union (ACLU) and the NAACP Legal Defense Fund are the leaders in the movement to abolish capital punishment.

Officials of these organizations are looking for volunteers.

Would it not be wonderful if history could record that the Christians of America in 1983´and 1984 were instrumental in stopping the executions of almost 1,200 persons, most of whom are the least educated and the most disadvantaged of all U.S. citizens.

PART VII

The Poor

Chapter 32

Refugees: Monumental Task

The recent large numbers of refugees from Indochina. Afghanistan and Cuba may be harbingers of long-range trends of significant proportions. Everything seems to suggest that vast migrations may well be forthcoming in the near future. A rapid increase in the size of human populations, the ready availability of international travel and political turbulence are forces that almost inevitably will produce refugees.

The United States has been in the forefront of providing for humanity's newest refugees. Between April 1975 and July 1980, Indochinese refugees resettled in the U.S. totaled 388,802, representing 44 per cent of the total resettled worldwide (886,553). Indeed, in recent years, the United States has been the world's largest receiver of refugees and immigrants for permanent resettlement and has accepted about twice as many as the rest of the world combined.

During the 1970s, immigration and refugee flows to the United States were at or near the highest levels ever experienced — including those years before 1920 when immigration was almost totally unrestricted.

In 1978, the last year for which official statistics are available, more than 600,000 legal immigrants and refugees were admitted. The figures cited for the 1970s do not include the undocumented illegal migrants, whose number is not certain.

The pressures to continue and even increase the numbers is intense. Mexico, the principal source of illegal migrants, is

First published in the *National Catholic Reporter*, May 22, 1981.

projected to add 60 million more people to its current population of 68 million in the next two decades. Mexico would have
to create 700,000 new jobs each year to prevent the already high
unemployment rate from rising; experts predict that Mexico
can at most reach half that number of new jobs.

The spectacular rise in the number of immigrants entering
the United States is not paralleled in other nations, where sharp
downward revisions in immigration quotas are the norm.

Early in 1981, the presidential commission established by the
Congress will report its recommendations as to what the United States should do to formulate a rational and coherent
immigration policy for the 1980s. This commission, chaired by
Father Theodore Hesburgh, will seek to make reasonable
recommendations, keeping in mind that the United States has
some humanitarian duty toward the world's 13 to 16 million
officially designated refugees.

In addition, the U.S. has some obligation to try to provide
asylum for persons who will voluntarily seek to migrate in
order to escape intolerable living conditions. At the same time,
the commission must keep in mind the intense depth of feeling
in the United States that we are already accepting too many
immigrants. A June 1980 Roper poll revealed that 80 per cent of
Americans want to reduce the number of legal immigrants who
can enter the United States each year.

The arguments suggesting that the U.S. needs more workers
to enhance its industrial productivity are not clear or cogent.
Even the most liberal voices in the United States become
xenophobic when they contemplate large numbers of immigrants taking relatively attractive jobs in the United States. At
the same time, there is a broad consensus in America that we
should sustain the long-standing U.S. value of openness to
immigrants and refugees from diverse sources.

There is also a consensus that genuine economic and social
development in the Third World is essential if we are to
diminish the pressures that produce refugees. Sophisticated
techniques of trade and aid with Mexico are particularly essential if the United States ever expects to control the flow of
illegal aliens crossing the Mexican border into the United
States.

Immigration should be a central component of this nation's foreign policy. The United States should neither encourage migration unreasonably nor neglect efforts to alleviate those refugee flows into Pakistan, the Sudan, Somalia and Thailand, where millions of human beings reside in circumstances unworthy of the human condition. The next president and the next Congress must confront this monumental task and continue to implement the United States' oldest moral tradition of being a haven for those who seek a new homeland.

Chapter 33

As U.S. Launches War Against Poor, Few Protest

Everywhere I talk to people they express their amazement that the United States is watching the launching of a war against the poor and is doing virtually nothing about it. Nothing like this has ever happened in America before. More than $30 billion is being taken out of social programs for the poor and is being transferred directly to the Pentagon. No one can deny that this is the objective reality. But the protests are small or muted and up to now without major significance.

Almost everyone I talked to also expects that demonstrations — even riots — will occur when the full impacts of the cuts in job training, Medicaid, food stamps and educational funding are felt at the local level.

Even the partisans of the Reagan administration, furthermore, do not see how the president's economic program is really supposed to work. Federal funding will not be cut back so the cure for inflation, allegedly derivable from a curtailment of federal spending, will not come from this source.

The 10 per cent tax cut during each of the next three years being urged by the Reagan administration also leaves people skeptical. The theory that the money will be saved and invested and thus increase capital formation rests on assumptions and premises that many feel are questionable or even fallacious. If the Congress refuses to give the administration the full three

First published in the *National Catholic Reporter*, May 22, 1981.

year proposal, the administration can fault the Congress if relief from inflation does not result. If, on the other hand, the Congress passes the essence of the Kemp-Roth bill, the administration will have to produce results or be exposed to several vulnerabilities.

But no matter what the ultimate result may be, the poor will be victimized. It is an unprecedented war against the poor now almost certain to be won. Why did the Reagan administration choose a wrenching of the poor as the core of its economic recovery plan?

One theory asserts that the Stockman-Reagan philosophy is simply callous and cruel. Stockman denies that people have entitlements. When Reagan states that he wants to get the government off the backs of the people, he means the white, wealthy people who elected him should pay lower taxes for the programs designed to help the poor and the disadvantaged. This theory may seem simplistic and harsh, but it is not without substance.

A second theory to explain the incredible war on the poor posits that the staff in the Reagan administration are true believers in the economic theories of right-wing economists and that in their sincere determination to cut back on federal expenditures, they have attacked the programs least familiar to them and those whose curtailment would draw the least resistance.

A third theory suggests that the Reagan administration, in slashing away $30 billion in social programs, is following a minority or perhaps a slim majority opinion within the United States which sincerely feels social welfare programs have made it too easy for persons to remain on unemployment compensation instead of working, have allowed food stamps to go to too many recipients and have permitted those less industrious persons to "free load" on the taxpayer. Study after study has demonstrated that these allegations are without substantial merit. But they are still believed — and now are being acted on by the White House.

Regardless of which theory or combination of theories one accepts to explain the savagery of the cuts, the ultimate fact is that the slashes are overwhelming, comprehensive and permanent. Several important developments will be wiped out as, for example, a measure passed almost unanimously by Congress last year which would extend to adopting parents of difficult to place children Medicaid and other benefits. There are in the United States about 500,000 children in a foster-care system. To promote the adoption of these homeless children, many of whom have medical or behavior problems, small grants equal to the welfare payment to which the child would otherwise be entitled were extended to adoptive parents. Last week, the Senate Finance Committee eliminated the adoption entitlement provision.

If impoverished children, without parents, are not among the "truly needy," it is difficult to know who is.

The statutes of the Plymouth Massachusetts colony, enacted soon after 1630, stipulated that "every township shall make competent provision for the maintenance of the poor." Has the nation in 1981 forgotten that early and fundamental principle of justice which has always been followed in U.S. life?

Chapter 34

To Preserve a Just and Compassionate Society

The statutes of the Plymouth Colony enacted in the 1630s stipulated that "every township shall make competent provision for the maintenance of the poor." It is significant that public responsibility for the welfare of the needy has been a feature of American government at some level since colonial times.

That responsibility is now being denied by the present administration. Incredibly the administration is apparently able to cut back almost 40 billion dollars in social programs. The statutes of the Plymouth Colony stated simply that the "poor" have a right to "maintenance." Now we are told that there are "truly needy" and then the others. We are led to believe that the "others" are lazy or deceptive or somehow unworthy of that aid which the United States has always given to those who are unable through no fault of their own to find adequate employment.

Within the past five months the administration in Washington has sought to destroy some of the finest programs enacted by a compassionate America over the past 50 years.

The National Council of Churches — a body which represents virtually all protestant churches in the United States, recently issued a sweeping message expressing its "fundamen-

Address at the Commencement Exercises of Boston State College, June 6, 1981.

tal disagreement" with the administration's policies. It expressed opposition to the administration's cutbacks in social spending, its energy policy, its hikes in military spending and parts of its foreign policy. The message of the National Council of Churches marked the first time since the establishment of this body in 1950 that the Council has issued such a broad condemnation of the policies of any administration.

Here is what the representatives of millions of Christians stated:

> In the administration's vision of America the fittest survive and prosper. And there is little room for public purpose since it interferes with private gain.

The administration, the National Council of Churches states, is rejecting a vision of America that "has deep roots in religious faith and biblical images of divine intent and human possibility."

Recently I was talking with a business official who said that the biggest challenge today is to "get government off our backs." But it turned out that this gentleman got his education under the G.I. Bill and started his business with a loan from the Small Business Administration. He also bought his home with the help of an FHA mortgage and lives in a suburb which was made possible by federal highway money and is subsidized by federal sewage grants. His parents are no burden to him thanks to Social Security and Medicare. His children, moreover, are in college on federal loans and grants.

When this corporate executive states that we should "get government off our backs" he means that we should cut back on food stamps, medical care for the needy and subsidized housing for the poor.

When pressed this affluent businessman says that the problems of society cannot be resolved "by throwing money at them." Apparently only the problems of the Pentagon can be solved by "throwing money at them."

Is it not unbelievable that some 40 billion dollars is being transferred from the poor to the Pentagon? It may be that this fact is so unbelievable that people have not yet been able to believe much less comprehend it. It is almost incomprehensible to contemplate that this administration projects that by 1986 the proposed cuts in social programs will add up to 320 billion dollars. In addition, it is unbelievable that the projected budget for the Pentagon will by 1986 experience a growth from its present level of 178 billion to 367 billion.

The impending cuts proposed by the administration in Washington and apparently to be acquiesced in by the Congress constitute a dark cloud over these otherwise joyous proceedings tonight.

The proposed cuts are disastrous and outrageous. Public transportation, for example, will be slashed by 23.2%, assistance to housing will be diminished by 33% and federal aid to elementary, secondary and vocational education will be reduced by 18.1%.

There will be in the next year alone a 25% reduction in most social programs. Of special relevance to students here and future students is the proposed cut in aid to college students which over the next five years will total 23 billion dollars!

These cuts will bring the most severe damage to the fulfillment of the mission and mandate of Boston State College, the oldest public institution of higher learning in the metropolitan city of Boston.

Boston State College educates 8,500 undergraduates and graduate students. By diligent recruitment and affirmative action of all kinds the minority student enrollment at Boston State College has increased so that it now represents 17% of the entire student body.

Those who are planning the drastic slashes in social programs do not understand that poverty continues to haunt at lest 27 million people in America, many of whom are elderly. Do they realize that about half of the 5 million older women who are living alone have yearly incomes of $3,000 or less? Do they realize that 25% of all women who are now working can expect to be poor in their old age? Middle-aged and older full-time homemakers, moreover, can expect to live their later years alone and in poverty. Three-fourths of all nursing home residents are women. The average age for widowhood in America is 56. Two-thirds of all widows live alone, and one-third live below the official poverty line.

All of these figures are even more grim when we speak of

black women. For blacks in general the economic gains of the 1960s were reversed in the 1970s. The disparity between the incomes of whites and blacks is nearly as wide today as it was when President Eisenhower came to the White House in 1953. In that year the median income of black families was 58% of that of whites. That figure increased to 65% during the Johnson administration but since then the gap has widened steadily and the most recent census tabulation shows that the median income of black families is now only 57% of that of white families.

Consequently it is enormously important for the federal government to do everything in its power to maximize opportunities for those who are disadvantaged by reason of poverty or of other circumstances. The whole thrust of the administration's proposals, however, goes in the opposite direction. The victims of the proposals will be the poor, the minorities and the women of America.

It is time now to begin a nationwide campaign and crusade made up of students, educators, parents and others who recognize that federal programs to eliminate poverty cannot succeed unless there are opportunities of all kinds for young people to acquire those skills in college which are essential if they are to liberate themselves from all of the disadvantages which through no fault of their own have surrounded their lives.

We must not yield to that sense of powerlessness which comes to us when we see that even progressive legislators have acquiesced in the most drastic slashes in social programs in the history of the nation. We are not powerless unless we allow ourselves to become so. We must not allow ourselves to be intimidated by those in high places who will brush aside every protest at the defunding of social programs by claiming that they have a mandate. This claim is being used to mute the criticism and to silence the opposition. It must not diminish our determination to protest the reversal of something very fundamental and sacred in American life.

What we are seeing in Washington is a reversal and a repudiation of that fundamental principle first enacted into American law by our forefathers in the Plymouth Colony. We still believe in that sacred principle set forth by the Pilgrims at

Plymouth when they mandated that there shall be "competent provision for the maintenance of the poor."

The graduates of 1981 have reason to be anxious and apprehensive as they view the anguish and agonies which this nation is now undergoing. There are many reasons to be even more apprehensive when we look out at the global village and see there the frightening challenges to our very existence. But we know that all of our hopes and aspirations for the alleviation of misery nationally and internationally can be realized because we believe in the mission of the United States. We know as citizens of America that we are unique and that we have a mission and a destiny not given to others.

Sometimes we wonder whether or not this is a dream which cannot be fulfilled. The words of Archibald MacLeish are reassuring:

> There are those who will say that the liberation of humanity, the freedom of man and mind, is nothing but a dream. They are right. It is the American dream.

Chapter 35

New Economics: The Fittest Survive

For the first time in its history, the United States has withdrawn billions of dollars in benefits for the poor. Thirty-two billion dollars have been slashed from food stamps, nutrition programs, rent subsidies and employment opportunities. Why? To test a theory to control inflation, which everyone concedes is a big gamble, an experiment and a program which has never worked in any other country!

All of the poor will be poorer. Every one of the 10 million persons living in subsidy housing will pay more rent. Everyone on food stamps will receive less. Every disadvantaged child will have fewer educational opportunities.

The figures are staggering. There will be 25 per cent fewer benefits for 900,000 low-income, disabled and elderly persons, 1.4 million handicapped persons will have their opportunities lessened. More than one million college students will have to pay more tuition.

The Reagan slashes in the budget are ephochal. They constitute a massive transfer of resources from the poor to the wealthy. The loss of opportunities for the poor may be permanent because of the sharp cutback in taxes for the corporations and the affluent. Corporate taxes may be on their way out. In 1960, 24 per cent of all federal tax revenues came from corporations; in 1970, 17 per cent. Under Reagan's proposal, this will decrease to 12 per cent . The projected loss in tax revenues during the next five years totals a staggering $750 billion!

First published in the *National Catholic Reporter*, August 14, 1981.

The next tax concessions are directed to the middle or upper class. Child-care credits, for example, are raised from $400 to $720 for a couple with one child and to $1,440 for a couple with two or more children. But the proposal to make the credits refundable in the case of poor, working parents who have no tax liability was dropped.

The revolutionary reduction of taxes apparently derives from a philosophy that the private sector and not the government should do more in social services. The *New York Times* August 2 editorialized that Reagan's "economic remedies are an assault on the very idea that free people can solve their collective problems through representative government."

Virtually every religious body in the United States opposed what Reagan and the Congress have done in the budget and tax initiatives. No one in Washington, to my knowledge, can recall any major domestic issue on which all of the religious groups were so unified.

Recently the National Council of Churches (NCC) — a body which represents virtually all Protestant churches in the United States — issued a sweeping message expressing "fundamental disagreement" with the Reagan administration policies. It expressed opposition to the administration's cutback in social spending and parts of its foreign policy. The NCC message marked the first time since the establishment of that board in 1950 that it has issued such a broad condemnation of any administration's policies.

The statement is sharp in its rebuke: "in the administration's vision of America, the fittest survive and prosper." The Administration, the NCC states, is rejecting a vision of America that "has deep roots in religious faith and biblical images of divine intent in human possibilities."

Twenty-seven million people in America still live under the poverty line. The budget and tax measures which will take effect October 1, 1981, can only hurt these individuals, the most vulnerable in our society.

Chapter 36

No, the U.S. is Disdainful

The radical shredding of America's humane programs and idealistic principles goes on at the hands of the Reagan administration. Recently in New Jersey during the gubernatorial campaign, Reagan told the voters that they had a "choice between those who think government spending and taxes are the solution to our problems and those ... who understand that government spending and over-taxation are the problem."

This is, of course, a caricature of both the liberal and the conservative philosophies of government. The liberals do not think government spending and taxes will solve all the nation's problems. Nor do conservatives — except possibly some extremists — think government spending and over-taxation constitute the major problems confronting the United States.

The real problems are entirely different — a decline in production, chronic inflation, unprecedented high interest rates, a lag in productive scientific research and excessive oil imports. Even if government spending diminished sharply and taxes were decreased, these problems would not go away. Because these issues are so complex and so intractable, one has to wonder whether the administration, by obsessively referring to government spending and taxes, is seeking to keep the public's mind off the real problems.

The administration is also applying perniciously over-

First published in the *National Catholic Reporter*, January 22, 1982.

simplified rhetoric to U.S. relations with the Third World. Reagan in effect told the underdeveloped nations that the United States believes in the alleged "magic of the market-place" and that they can expect the United States will continue to rank no better than 15th among the 17 nations that share their resources with the Third World.

Indeed disdain on the Third World more and more characterizes the attitude of the Reagan administration at the United Nations. The White House's representative in Geneva cast a vote against the World Health Organization's program to monitor ads for infant formulas because Reagan thinks this would infringe on the rights of U.S. corporations. The administration postponed —perhaps indefinitely — the adoption of a proposed code for a law of the seas because under that proposal the powerful nations — and especially the United States — would have to cooperate with the 77 nonaligned nations in bringing about a global plan for the exploitation of those seabed minerals which surely belong to mankind and not the super-powers or the multinational corporations.

United Nations Ambassador Jeane Kirkpatrick recently expressed contempt for the aspirations of developing nations. To her they represent anti-American feelings, which she resents almost to the point of being vindictive. On the new public television program of Ben Wattenberg, Kirkpatrick asserted vehemently that the nonaligned nations must learn that they will have to "pay a price" for being nonaligned against the United States.

Such hostility to the hopes and aspirations of more than 100 nations in the UN general assembly can only deepen the antagonism these countries feel toward the United States. The bitterness contained in Kirkpatrick's statements about the nonaligned nations demonstrates that she and the Reagan administration have an attitude toward the UN which contradicts the spirit if not the letter of the messages of all the popes who have spoken to the United Nations since its founding in 1945.

The Carter administration sought to have the United States admired and applauded at the UN. The Reagan administration seems consciously determined to alienate those poorer nations that make up an automatic majority of the general assembly of the UN.

Such hostility by the United States can only breed and bring trouble. This is especially true in the 51 nations of Africa. This continent of 350 million people now has only four million whites residing on it — all in South Africa. If the blacks of Africa perceive U.S. foreign policy as being formulated because of the interest of South Africa's whites — as they understandably could — the antagonism they will harbor may perdure for a long time.

The anti-American rhetoric of sometimes bellicose poor nations is not easy to take — at the UN or elsewhere. But the rhetoric will not be softened until the United States removes the several causes of it. The nations that indulge in anti-American sentiments feel toward the United States like the 13 colonies felt toward England: exploited, cheated, dominated. They want a new international economic order and are prepared to fight for it. They desire a "new relationship of dignity and respect, not one of docility and servility," as Father Miguel D'Escoto, foreign minister of Nicaragua, recently told Assistant Secretary of State Thomas O. Enders in Managua.

President Carter took the UN seriously. He is the only president to urge the U.S. Senate to ratify the four major UN treaties which the United States alone among major nations has refused to ratify. Carter was humiliated by the fact that of the 19 major UN covenants or treaties, the United States Senate has ratified only the five least controversial.

There is a strong anti-government bias in the approach of the Reagan administration. Government is regularly ridiculed. It is portrayed as the source of problems rather than a place for their resolution. This anti-government emphasis is now being carried into the United Nations. There capitalism is exalted, the multinational corporations are endowed with magical qualities and mankind is told that only free enterprise will bring freedom. Will the next step be a proposal by the Reagan administration that the UN dismantle its specialized agencies? This would be consistent with the anti-government policies followed by the administration in slashing domestic social programs and curbing the regulatory agencies.

Kirkpatrick recently stated that the foreign policy of the Reagan administration toward the Third World is "substantially different" from that of the last two or three administrations.

Are we seeing the carrying out of Adam Smith in an extreme form? Or is it the beginning of a new anarchy?

Chapter 37

Young Amerasians Deserve Better

At a time when many Americans lament the demise of detente and the resistance of the White House to the enforcement of international human rights, there is nonetheless reason to be proud that the United States has, since the fall of Saigon, transported 502,000 persons from Southeast Asia to American shores where they will have the right to become citizens.

Tragically, however, those persons to whom the United States owes the most have been left behind — the children in Southeast Asia whose fathers are American GIs. These Amerasians number up to 25,000 in Vietnam. There are 6,000 in Korea, at least 4,500 in Thailand and 5,000 in the Philippines.

The burdens on these youngsters are heavy. They are clearly identifiable and are scorned — especially in those Asian nations which determine legal rights by patrimonial lines. Their marriage prospects are minimal. Children whose fathers are American blacks suffer particular disadvantages.

At least some of these half-Americans are still being born in Korea. The laws of that nation state that it is a criminal and civil offense to make a Korean woman pregnant under promise of marriage. But U.S. servicemen are seldom prosecuted on this charge because, by agreement of the Korean government, jurisdiction on charges of a criminal nature against a U.S. citizen pass to American authorities 15 days after the charges are introduced. Under U.S. law, fathering a child is not a criminal offense. And even if a father is ordered to make financial compensation to the mother of his child, this obliga-

First published in the *National Catholic Reporter*, June 4, 1982.

tion is virtually extinguished once the GI leaves Korea.

The United States is the only country which has turned its back on children in this predicament. In the days of the colonial powers, the illegitimate children of English, Dutch or French men were given a legal right to elect citizenship in the land of their fathers. In Paris there is a large community of Vietnamese including a significant number of persons of Franco-Vietnamese parentage.

An attempt to create a right to American citizenship for half-Americans in Southeast Asia is embodied in a bill (H.R. 808) filed by Congressman Stewart McKinney (R-Conn.) and in S. 1698 by Senator Jeremiah Denton (R-Ala.). These bills would allow children born after 1950 of American fathers who reside in Korea or Vietnam, Laos or Thailand to have the same right to come to the United States as married or unmarried children of two American parents. The bills would also permit individual Americans the legal right to sponsor these youngsters — a right denied in practice under existing immigration law.

The bill would not increase the number of people on welfare in the United States, as it would require that the sponsors be legally and financially responsible for five years. Nor would the bill actually increase the number of immigrants, because the Amerasians who wanted to enter the United States would be among the 20,000 already coming from the nations in question under existing law.

Several organizations are working for the enactment of this legislation. No one has worked more diligently than Maryknoll Father Alfred V. Keane, who for 25 years served in Inchon, South Korea, the thousands of children of Korean-American parentage in that country. Keane is America's most articulate advocate of the McKinney-Denton bills.

The ravages of the Vietnam war to the American soul and spirit are so omnipresent and so overwhelming that the almost irresistible tendency is to put that war out of one's mind completely. The thousands of half-American children — many now approaching young adulthood — who were abandoned by their fathers in Southeast Asia deserve and demand our compassion and our action.

Chapter 38

Cast Ballot in U.S. for Poor Nations

On July 2, 1983, after almost a month of meetings in Belgrade, Yugoslavia, the 3,000 delegates from 164 countries adjourned the sixth quadrennial meeting of the United Nations Conference on Trade and Development (UNCTAD). They were more disappointed and discouraged than at any time since these meetings started 24 years ago.

The Third World came to Belgrade with firm and documented proposals that the industrialized nations share their new economic recovery with the underdeveloped countries. They called on the West to provide more aid to the developing world, increase World Bank and International Monetary Fund (IMF) credit, agree to new ways to stabilize the prices of raw materials, reduce the staggering burden of the Third World's debt of $700 billion and diminish protectionist measures that discriminate against the exports of poorer countries.

The package would increase the earnings of the Third World by about $70 billion during the next 24 months. If that occurred, the delegates from the Third World argued, the economic recovery in the industrialized world would be deepened.

Western industrialized countries, fortified by the negative attitude of the United States, rejected all of the demands of the Third World as unrealistic or as technically beyond the conference's jurisdiction. At all previous UNCTAD conferences, the rich and poor nations were able to come to some paper agree-

First published in the *National Catholic Reporter*, August 26, 1983.

ment which if not satisfactory did not intensify the anger of the poor nations. But this year the poor countries are leaving in anger and frustration.

The group of 77 — the nonaligned nations —expressed the anger of the poorer nations in a resolution against America's economic boycott of Nicaragua. By a vote of 81-18, with seven abstentions, the conference condemned all "trade restrictions, blockades, embargoes and economic sanctions" taken by rich countries against the developing world. Although the United States is not specifically named, the resolution was promoted by the Reagan administration's decision to deprive Nicaragua of the right to sell most of its sugar crop in the United States. Sugar is Nicaragua's fourth largest export crop and almost all of it has been exported to the United States. The poor nations were also angry that the United States vetoed the $2.2 million granted by the Inter-American Development Bank to build roads in Nicaragua. The other 42 South American members of the bank voted in favor of the loan.

The Reagan administration, while cutting back in economic aid to several nations, recently doubled military aid to several Sub-Saharan African nations. In 1980 all military aid to Sub-Saharan Africa totaled $78 million; $201 million has been requested for 1984. At the same time the administration is working against an amendment proposed by the foes of apartheid in the Congress that would bar the United States from voting in favor of a $1 billion loan from the IMF to South Africa.

Economic aid has not been popular in the Congress in recent years. It can be passed only when packaged with military aid or almost disguised as a form of security assistance. But the needs of the poorer nations for all types of economic and financial help from the rich nations grow more compelling and urgent each day. Cyrus Vance in his recent book *Hard Choices* reminded us that "each day there are over 200,000 new mouths to feed in the world" and that "by the year 2000 the world will have an additional 1.5 billion people" — with 90 per cent of that increase in the developing nations.

The scarcity of news about the UNCTAD conference is undoubtedly an indication of the indifference and the callousness of the rich nations toward the poor. The appropriate Christian approach to the poor is stated in the special liturgy for the United States for the Fourth of July. The opening prayer is as follows:

> Let national boundaries not set limits to our concern. Ward off the pride that comes from worldly wealth and power. Give us the courage to open ourselves in love, to the service of all your people.

As the issues emerge for the election to occur November 6, 1984, we can hope and pray that there will be a significant number of U.S. voters who will make a candidate's position on economic aid to poor nations an essential norm by which they evaluate his worthiness to be the next president of the richest nation in the history of the world.

Chapter 39

Help Affect Decisions on Budget

Even for the politically sophisticated, the federal budget proposed for fiscal year 1985 is somewhat incomprehensible. It also appears to be morally indefensible. How can any government spend $925.5 billion and charge $180.4 billion of it to a future generation to pay?

If such an extreme measure (never before proposed by any president in 200 years) were for only one year, it might be defensible. But the deficits in 1986 and 1987 are projected to be the same $180 billion or higher.

The proposed budget contains an increase of $71.8 billion — more than half of it for the Pentagon, whose budget would rise to the incredible amount of $305 billion, an after-inflation increase of 13 per cent. This figure contrasts sharply with reductions of about three per cent in spending for vocational education for the handicapped, adult education and the social service block grant. Other measures targeted for cuts include food stamps, housing assistance, energy aid and other low-income programs.

It is significant that the administration ignored recommendations of its own commission on hunger and would, in effect, force about 500,000 people off the rolls of the feeding program for women, infants and children.

The proposed slashes in social programs could have been more drastic. But there seems to be slight hope that Congress in an election year could secure the votes to bring back the

First published in the *National Catholic Reporter*, February 10, 1984.

173

spending level on domestic programs to the point where all needy people would be protected.

The unprecedented deficit and the squeeze on programs for the indigent did not deter the White House from seeking to finance its own obsessions and the recommendations of the Kissinger Commission for Central America. A staggering $2.8 billion is proposed for Central America for the next four years.

Even the best-informed observers of the national scene will get weary as the budget makes its way through Congress. What can an ordinary citizen do to influence crucial decisions in the months ahead?

The first answer is to reemphasize that no one can really be a good Christian if he or she is not a good citizen. And being a good citizen means one participates actively and aggressively. There are many ways to do this — making one's view known to Congress, to the media and to one's friends and community.

An effective way to supplement such efforts is by vigorous collective action in public interest organizations, such as Bread for the World, Common Cause, Network and similar groups. In the past several months, organizations such as these helped to blunt some of the worst administration proposals to cut back aid for nutrition and education programs. The efforts of citizens' groups will be needed even more urgently in the next few months when the pressure to lower the deficit could result in tragic cutbacks in programs for the needy.

The United States is confronted for the first time in at least 50 years with an administration that wants to repudiate the compassion for the unfortunate that the nation has come to expect from its government. One more manifestation of that lack of compassion was evident in President Reagan's remarks on ABC's "Good Morning America" show January 31. Asked about the contention that his policies were causing misery, the president replied incoherently and incorrectly as follows:

> What we have found in this country, and maybe we're more aware of it now, is one problem that we've had, even in the best of times, and that is the people who are sleeping on the grates, the homeless who are homeless, you might say, *by choice* (emphasis added).

The White House later tried to justify the president's callous remark by saying that 25 per cent of the homeless refused help from governmental agencies.

The budget proposed for 1985 represents the choices of an administration ready to attack Congress for being soft on defense and hard on taxes. It leaves Congress members, anxious about their reelection on November 6, with tormenting choices.

Citizens who desire to be good Christians have an obligation to make their opinions known to those elected to represent them. Individual and collective initiatives by citizens could have a profound effect on the policies this nation will elect to follow during the next 250 days.

PART VIII

Soviet Jews/Israel

Chapter 40

Cultural Genocide Being Waged Against Jews of the Soviet Union

Mr. Speaker, as a sponsor of the proposal before us to place the US Congress on record as opposing the cultural genocide being waged against the Jews of the Soviet Union, I rise to urge its enactment.

This concurrent resolution, Mr. Speaker, expresses in clear and brief language our commitment to human dignity and religious freedom and our absolute refusal to tolerate that kind of religious persecution which has already cast a grotesque scare on the history of our time.

The operative language of this resolution is as follows:

Resolved by the House of Representatives (the Senate concurring), That it is the sense of Congress that the President of the United States of America shall take immediate and determined steps to —

(1) call upon the Soviet Government to permit the free expression of ideas and the exercise of religion by all its citizens in accordance with the Soviet Constitution; and

(2) utilize formal and informal contacts with Soviet officials in an effort to secure an end to discrimination against religious minorities; and

(3) request of the Soviet Government that it permit its citizens the right to emigrate from the Soviet Union to the countries of their choice as affirmed by the United Nations Declaration of Human Rights; and

First published in the *Congressional Record*, April 17, 1972.

(4) raise in the General Assembly of the United Nations the issue of the Soviet Union's transgression of the Declaration of Human Rights, particularly against Soviet Jews and other minorities.

Mr. Speaker, I have been invited to go to Israel next month as a consulting fact-finder on behalf of the National Interreligious Consultation on Soviet Jewry. I hope that on that occasion I will be able to bring with me the message that here in the United States, our highest legislative body has proclaimed unequivocally its opposition to the persecution of the Soviet Jews, by enacting this resolution.

I wish to insert at this point in the Record, Mr. Speaker, the text of my testimony before our Committee on Foreign Affairs in Support of this bill:

Mr. Chairman, I greatly appreciate this opportunity to present my views on the conditions which confront the Jews of the Soviet Union. Your committee is performing an excellent public service in its deliberations on this situation.

I pray that the experience of the Jews in the 20th century — and indeed, the experience of persecution of Jews over 5,000 years — will never be forgotten. Anti-semitism is a malignancy which is periodically suppressed, but unless we are constantly vigilant, it will proliferate. Unless Americans of every background and, particularly, those of us in Congress, bring to the attention of people throughout the world the plight of Soviet Jewry, we shall pay a terrible price for our negligence.

A dispatch from Moscow in the November 14, 1971, *New York Times* by Hedrick Smith contined the following account:

> Striding along the treelined streets of the Moldavian capital of Kishinev a few days ago, a Jewish chemist quietly described how his fervent desire to emigrate to Israel was frustrated by fear. If he applied for an exit visa, he said, he might lose his job, and there would be trouble for his wife and two small daughters.
>
> In a Ukrainian city, members of a large Jewish family complained that they had been waiting eight years to get out of their cramped, one room apartment. When new apart-

ments become available, they said, Jews never seem to get them.

Accounts such as these are typical of the often-subtle, often-obvious discrimination levied against Jews by government agencies in the Soviet Union.

A constituent of mine who recently returned from an extensive tour of the Soviet Union reported that he had enormous difficulty in making contact with Soviet Jews. "They fear to talk with Americans in public places, or even in their own homes," he said, "because they have reason to believe that secret service agents are watching and listening."

Secret Practices

Some Americans who travel in Russia have adopted the practice of secretly depositing ritual prayer shawls and copies of the Hebrew scriptures in Russian synagogues. Ritual objects of the Jewish faith are systematically destroyed by anti-Jewish elements in the Soviet Union.

Jewish synagogues have been closed, and only a comparative few remain. More than 90 percent of the remaining synagogues have no rabbis today because there is no Jewish seminary for training rabbis. The few remaining rabbis are old men in their seventies and eighties.

In his excellent study, *Soviet Jewry Today and Tomorrow* (New York: Macmillan Co., 1971), the distinguished correspondent Boris Smolar reports that the Jewish heritage in Russia is being extinguished:

> On the whole, it can be said that the average young Jew in the Soviet Union feels like an orphan who is eager to find out more about the parents he has never seen. There is very little that his father or mother can tell him about the meaning of being a Jew, because most of the Jewish parents in the USSR today are either Soviet-born themselves or they were raised under the Soviet regime. He looks, therefore, to his Jewish grandparents for Jewish guidance — if they are still alive.

Those of us in the Congress who have long supported heavy pressures by our Government to make the Kremlin change its policies with respect to Jewish emigration continue to be appalled by the callousness of the Soviet regime. Notwithstanding the unequivocal language of article 13, paragraph 2 of the United Nations Declaration on Human Rights — officially ratified by the Soviet Union — that "everyone has the right to leave any country, including his own," Soviet Jews are simply not permitted to leave, at least not in substantial numbers.

At a time when prison reform is becoming a high national priority in our country, we should pause and reflect on the effective imprisonment of Soviet Jews. As our Supreme Court has forcefully indicated in *Kent* v. *Dulles* and a long line of other decisions, the freedom to travel outside of one's own country is a fundamental human right. Forbidden to leave Russia, the Soviet Jews are, in effect, incarcerated in a place where for the most part, they are the victims of invidious class discrimination.

State Department Views

I realize that State Department employees have come before your committee and said, in effect, that there is no pervasive anti-Jewish discrimination in Russia. Such statements, I submit, are untrue and reflect badly upon our government. I recognize that we are currently engaged in complex negotiations with the Soviet Union. And I realize President Nixon wants nothing to detract from the success of his planned trip to the Soviet Union. And I realize that the SALT talks are in a critical phase. However, the State Department and other federal agencies, in their attempts to keep the Kremlin at ease, have bent the truth to the point of obliteration.

To those who claim there is no systematic discrimination against the Soviet Jews, I would present Boris Smolar's account of employment opportunities for a Jew in Russia:

> The Soviet economic machine, in need of all kinds of labor, no longer makes any distinction between Jew and non-Jew, as was the case during the latter years of the Stalin

regime, or even in the early years of the Khrushchev regime. Promotion of Jews to higher positions is a different thing. This may explain why Jewish engineers. . .feel they do not receive the same recognition they see given to others.

Months ago I joined with Congressman William Ryan and many others of our colleagues in a resolution urging inclusion of Yiddish broadcasts over the Voice of America. The evidence is clear that a substantial portion of Soviet Jews speak Yiddish as their principal or secondary language. Yiddish broadcasts, even if only a few minutes a day, would indicate in a concrete way our compassion and warm feelings toward the Soviet Jews.

It was a very modest request.

Although it is hard to believe, the Director of the U.S. Information Agency, Mr. Shakespeare, and high-level representatives of the State Department refused to comply. They summoned a variety of largely misleading and irrelevant data in their arguments. At briefings, they stated and implied that Yiddish broadcasts, no matter how innocuous in content, were inconsistent with our Government's policy of not disturbing the Kremlin.

Is this the moral fiber which characterizes American history? Is this the broad dissemination of differing points of view piously claimed by the Voice of America? I think not.

Mr. Chairman, I believe that in matters affecting the social status of an ethnic or religous group in any country, we must speak out when there is pervasive injustice. The evidence of such injustice in the case of the Soviet Jews is overwhelming. If we fail here to protest, then we will have made a mockery of those principles upon which our nation was founded. The lesson of Nazi Germany must never be forgotten: If we ignore this problem it most certainly will not go away. By enlisting the force of world opinions against class discrimination in Russia, we can hope to get results. History demonstrates that the Russians are at least as sensitive to our opinion of them as we are to their opinion of us.

Five Specific Demands

I therefore urge our Government to endorse the five specific demands upon the Soviet Government made by the American Jewish Conference on Soviet Jewry:

1. To permit Jews throughout the USSR freely to develop Jewish communal and religious life and institutions and to associate and work with comparable Jewish communities and religious groups inside and outside the Soviet Union.

2. To make available the educational institutions, schools, teachers, textbooks, and scholarly materials necessary to teach Soviet Jews the heritage, the languages, the history, the beliefs, the practices, and the aspirations of the Jewish people.

3. To permit its Jewish citizens freely to practice, enhance, and perpetuate their culture and religion by the establishment of appropriate institutions including places of worship, and other religious facilities, theaters, publishing houses, newspapers, and journals, and to remove all discriminatory measures designed to restrict this freedom.

4. To use all means at its disposal to eradicate anti-Semitism and discrimination against individual Jews and to require, as the first step in this program, the immediate cessation of the virulent antisemitic propaganda that has suffused the Soviet mass media since the Six-Day War between the Arabs and Israel in 1967.

5. To permit Soviet Jewish families, many of whom were separated as a result of the Nazi holocaust, to be reunited with their brethren abroad and to implement the Kosygin promise of family reunion.

These demands are just. They were first promulgated several years ago and were adopted on February 25, 1971, by the World Conference of Jewish Communities on Soviet Jewry, held in Brussels. The conference was attended by 750 Jewish leaders from 27 countries, and was addressed by, among others, former Justice Arthur Goldberg, and David Ben Gurion, former Prime Minister of Israel.

Mr. Chairman, I applaud your committee's concern with these problems and I appreciate this opportunity to express my views.

Chapter 41

Freedom Versus Tyranny: The Jewish Struggle

Ever since the completion of Faneuil Hall on September 10, 1742, outcries against tyranny and pleas for freedom have echoed in this hall. Upon this rostrum have stood most of the most famous statesmen and orators of America.

It was in Faneuil Hall that the people of Massachusetts voted against the iniquitous stamp act. When British troops had been ordered to Boston a convention of representatives of nearly every town in Massachusettes convened at Faneuil Hall and met in this room for one week. It was on November 5, 1773 that the first of a series of meetings about the tea situation was held in Faneuil Hall. It was here that George Washington as the first President in 1789 proclaimed freedom and it was in this very hall that Wendell Phillips startled his audience with his famous speech against slavery.

For 200 years the people of Massachusetts have been coming to Faneuil Hall whenever they are troubled about threats to their freedoms. It was here that the people of this commonwealth protested the slanders of Senator Joseph McCarthy, proclaimed their solidarity with the freedom movement of the 1960's and protested the barbarism of America's war in Vietnam.

It is here today in this historic hall that we are gathered to protest the recurrence of the historic scourge of anti-Semitism.

Address given to the National Executive Committee of the Anti-Defamation League in Faneuil Hall, Boston, Massachusetts, May 29, 1976.

We are here also to proclaim the first freedom movement in the modern world — the rise and flowering of Zionism.

We sadly recall that neither the holocaust nor three decades of Zionism in action in Israel have eliminated basic anti-Semitism in the world. On May 26, 1976, a poll taken of 2,084 West Germans revealed that about half of the 60 million inhabitants of this nation have at least latent anti-Semitic tendencies. The anti-Jewish feeling was not limited to marginal or extremist political groups. The poll, conducted at Cologne University, indicated that some 30 percent of the population had latent prejudices against Jews which were capable of taking a violent form. The poll revealed that West Germans exaggerated almost ten-fold the number of Jews in that nation. The average answer of those polled stated that there were 268,000 Jews in West Germany; the total is just 26,000.

Anti-Zionism is the New Anti-Semitism

It is unbelievable that 28 years after the creation of Israel 72 nations of the earth could vote for the proposition that Zionism is a form of racism. It is incredible and shattering that representatives of nations with more than 60 percent of the world's population could categorize Zionism, a movement for moral liberation, as a "form of racism and racial discrimination."

We must be disturbed at the fallout effect of this resolution in the 72 nations which subscribed to it. But is there also a fallout from the global feeling against Zionism in the United States? On March 23, 1976, Spiro Agnew by implication stated that the Zionist dream as incarnate in Israel does not really deserve the support of the American people. The country and the Congress support Israel, Agnew would have us believe, because of an allegedly large number of Jews in "the three networks, the two wire services, the two pollsters and their organization, the New York Times and the Washington Post...and the news weeklies, Time and Newsweek..." Agnew continues his fantasy by alleging that foreign aid goes to Israel because of "the influence of the Zionist lobby."

Agnew continued his crude anti-Semitism by alleging that

"Israel has now embarked on an imperialistic exercise occupying Arab lands, the West Bank of the Jordan, the Golan Heights, the Gaza Strip, bringing about a police state in these areas..."

To those who are offended by Agnew's remarks, he adds insult to injury by claiming that "the trouble with the American Jewish community is that it is ultrasensitive." Agnew concluded his diatribe by asserting that the Anti-Defamation League of B'nai B'rith always characterizes as "bigotry" any "legitimate criticism of the Jewish community."

It is easy indeed to dismiss these charges as the ravings of a totally discredited person. But could the Agnew assault on the media and the Israeli lobby be the new way by which many Americans might express their anti-Semitic, anti-Israel and anti-Zionist prejudices?

As never before, Americans — especially Christian Americans — must reassess the fundamental reasons why the United States has a unique and profound alliance with Israel. Several political reasons come to mind quickly. Israel is a fighter for freedom in an area of the world where the United States needs strength and stability. Israel is a democratic state in a sea of totalitarian nations suspectible to the blandishments of the Kremlin.

However valid these reasons may be, the alliance of America with tiny Israel rests in the ultimate analysis on the moral and religious links which America has with the one nation in human history whose mission has been the ingathering of its exiles.

America has recognized from the very beginning of Israel the undeniable truth that Zionism is one of the noblest and deepest movements for liberation in modern times. Zionism is more than a political movement; it is an expression of worldwide Jewish religious beliefs and hopes.

Zionism is a profoundly held spiritual conviction of Jewish fidelity to the biblical covenant which links a people, a faith and a land in a unique religious and mystical unity.

It is not for a Christian to state whether or not Zionism and Judaism are theologically separable. But politically they cannot be separated. Zionism is the mystique, the "elan vital" of Israel. To equate Zionism with racism represents a frontal assault against the core values of Judaism. Consequently, the assertion of the alleged connection between Zionism and racism constitutes a new form of anti-Semitism.

Traditional anti-Semitism denied the individual Jew his personhood; this new anti-Semitism seeks to deny the Jewish people its nationhood.

In the debate which led to the UN resolution on November 10, 1975, equating Zionism with racism, Ambassador Baroody, of Saudi Arabia, stated that he had "no quarrel with Judaism — but with Zionism." The representative of Kuwait asserted that Zionism, born as a political movement in 1897, is not inherent in the theology of Judaism.

One wonders whether attempts to discredit Zionism while pretending to be respectful of Judaism will become the vogue in America and elsewhere with those who want to quarrel with Israel about the West Bank, the Palestinians or the theocratic characteristics of the Israeli nation.

For those who desire Israelis to have that freedom to which they are entitled as a country created by the United Nations the vindication of the validity of Zionism has now become an imperative duty. If Zionism with its religious and political implications, is not understood, there will be more and more individuals who will demand that Israel de-Zionize its culture and its legal institutions. These persons will claim that they are not against the State of Israel but only want it to be a secular democracy. In a certain sense, persons who insist that Israel conform itself to their own concepts of a value-free government are unwittingly robbing Israel of its heritage and despoiling it of its most precious legacy. Indeed, any formal call for Israel to disassociate itself from Zionism is a violation of Article I of the Charter of the United Nations, which is to promote and encourage respect "for human rights and for fundamental freedoms for all without distinction as to race, sex, language or religion."

If American opinion follows world opinion and turns against Israel under the code name Zionism, America will have turned its back on the three million Jews of Israel, the three million Jews in the USSR and every other Jew around the world. To debase, degrade or or dismiss Zionism as irrelevant or irrational is a rejection and a repudiation of Judaism.

Even in its most de-theologized or secularized manifestations Zionism expresses the noble dream of the ingathering of the exiles in the land of Israel. Zionism, even in its purely political form, cannot be separated from that fidelity to Judaism which brought about the massacre of European Jewry — fully one-third of the Jewish people.

It is apparently becoming evermore fashionable to issue calls for the de-Zionization of Israel. Such a call is sometimes preceded by the contention that Zionism is an anachronism.

The fact is that post-holocaust Jews with a "never again" determination obtained their motivation for their victories in Israel in both spirit and technology from Zionism. Zionism, it has been said, is the Jewish reassertion of manhood. Zionism demonstrated the inexhaustibility of the timeless message and meaning of the Bible.

In the 3,000 years since the term Zion was first placed in the sacred literature of the Jewish people, the concept of Zion has grown to symbolize and signify the very essence of Judaism. Those who, like Spiro Agnew, dismiss or downgrade the essential links between Zionism and Israel are not really different in their positions from the 72 nations that condemn Zionism as a form of racism. Ambassador Chaim Herzog, of Israel, noted in the UN debate about Zionism that "the world was witnessing the first organized attack on an established religion since the Middle Ages."

The freedom from tyranny which we assert today in historic Faneuil Hall is the very essence of the dream and vision of Zionism. Theodor Herzl, in 1897, viewed Zionism as the one way which Jews could escape the tyranny and oppression of the ghettos and the pogroms of 20 centuries. Zionism, both politically and religiously, is the implementation of the ancient Jewish hope for independence, freedom, and redemption.

Americans in their bicentennial year can understand the dream and realization of Zionism. In countless ways, Israel, like America, is a nation of refugees and pioneers living in a nation that is boundless in development.

America, like Israel, is a nation that cherishes freedom for itself and also aspires to make freedom possible for the rest of mankind. For these reasons — and countless others — Americans identify with Israel beause Israel reminds us of the best in ourselves. Israel reminds us of all the lost horizons, all the broken promises, all the shattered dreams, all the things that we never did that we should have done.

It seems impossible that the unique alliance which has existed for 28 years between the United States and Israel should erode in any way. Indeed, it seems inconceivable that this friendship should even be reassessed or renegotiated. The only thing to reassess is the depth of the moral dimensions of the relationship between the United States and Israel. Those dimensions are profound, perpetual and pervasive. Our commitment and promise to Israel was made before America's policy of the containment of communism was formulated. America's commitment to Israel has remained unquestioned through six presidencies and 14 Congresses.

In this bicentennial year, let us hope that the harmony and the friendship which has existed for three decades between America and Israel will perdure for at least another 200 years!

Chapter 42

Helsinki's Broken Promises

We can be certain that 1977 will constitute a crucial turning point in the life of the Helsinki Accord. At the Helsinki Conference in August 1975, President Ford said: "History will judge this conference not by what we say today, but by what we do tomorrow, not by the promises we make, but by the promises we keep." Since that time, it has become increasingly clear that the Soviet Union does not intend to keep its promises to permit full religious and cultural freedom and to allow its citizens the fundamental human right to rejoin their families abroad. The Soviet government has apparently adopted a policy of ignoring the human-rights provisions of the Helsinki Final Act, unless international pressure forces compliance. Now is clearly the time to exert such pressure.

Since the ratification of the Helsinki Accord, each positive step taken by the Soviet authorities has been matched by one or more negative actions. The modest reduction in the exorbitantly expensive emigration fee was matched by a steep increase in the tax on parcels received from abroad. This policy, adopted last June, was clearly aimed at the more than 1,000 Jewish families who applied for permission to emigrate, lost their jobs as a result, and now require these parcels in order to support themselves and their families. The number of Jews and others permitted to emigrate has not increased. The systematic harassment of those who apply for exit visas and passports continues. In October, authorities brutally beat and

Keynote Address to the Second National Interreligious Consultation on Soviet Jewry at the University of Chicago, November 29, 1976.

arrested a number of Soviet Jews peacefully protesting Soviet policy.

Even in this action, however, the Soviet government demonstrated that it is by no means immune to pressure from abroad. The mass arrests precipitated a great deal of criticism from the West. Along with other elected officials and citizens of the United States, I expressed my outrage to Soviet officials. A subsequent announcement — that two of those imprisoned would not be released but would be prosecuted for a criminal offense carrying a prison term of five years — provoked a second wave of protest. The Soviet government dropped the charges and released the two men. This was the first instance in which criminal charges against dissident Soviet Jews did not result in trial, conviction and imprisonment. Intense international pressure clearly had some effect.

In the coming year, we must seize other opportunities to focus world attention on the Soviet Union's failure to adhere to the human-rights provisions of the Helsinki Accord. We must apply organized, systematic and continuing pressure. The congressionally created Commission on Security and Cooperation in Europe has begun to exercise its responsibility to monitor, evaluate and report on compliance with the Helsinki Accord. Under the terms of the legislation that created the commission, the President is required to report to the Congress and the nation every six months on progress toward fulfillment of the goals and duties set by the Helsinki Final Act. The commission's activities and the presidential reports present us with new opportunities to emphasize the importance of the Helsinki Agreement and the USSR's inexcusable failure to comply with it.

President-elect Carter has stated his profound interest in international human rights in general and the plight of Soviet Jews in particular. He has also declared his firm intention to place America's traditional concern for individual liberty and human rights at the core of our nation's foreign policy. On November 24 William Scranton, US ambassador to the United Nations, criticized the USSR's failure to adhere to the Helsinki Accord. At a speech before a UN General Assembly committee, Scranton warned the Soviet Union that the new administration would insist that Moscow live up to its promises on the free movement of people and ideas in considering "further normalization of relations with the Soviet sphere." He charged that the Soviet Union had engaged in destructive efforts to discredit the principles of individual human freedom, and he criticized the UN for its insensitivity to the USSR's "denial of freedom of thought, religious freedom, and emigration to its own citizens."

The incoming administration will, one hopes, elevate the human-rights provisions of the Helsinki Accord to a prominent position on the agenda of East-West relations, as part of our nation's fundamental commitment to the free movement of people and ideas. The US and other nations should press for a thorough discussion of this issue in the UN.

Still another opportunity to focus world attention on the human-rights section of the Helsinki Accord is presented by the first conference to review the Helsinki Act, scheduled to convene in Belgrade, Yugoslavia, in September 1977. A preliminary meeting to set the agenda for the conference will take place in June. The USSR will undoubtedly attempt to demonstrate that it has complied with the agreement and to narrow the focus of the conference. The United States and the other Western signatories must be prepared to point out the Soviet Union's failure to live up to its obligations, and must draw the world's attention to the brutal denial of human rights in the USSR The Belgrade Conference of all 35 nations which signed the Helsinki Agreement can serve as a forum to communicate to the Soviet Union and the rest of the world America's deep commitment to human rights.

In this context, it is essential that the US comply fully with the terms of the Helsinki Final Act. To the extent that we are in violation of any of the act's provisions, our moral position vis-a-vis the Soviet Union is compromised.

Unfortunately, there are several respects in which the US is at least arguably in violation of the accord. The McCarran Act, which prohibits alleged communists from emigrating to the US and the State Department's authority to prevent certain individuals from visiting the country are unjust and unnecessary laws which could be construed as violating the Helsinki Final

Act. We must not undermine our ability to call for strict adherence to the terms of the accord by retaining such policies.

When I was in the Soviet Union last year, a young man who had tried unsuccessfully to emigrate to Israel and lost his job as a result told me, "If it were not for the Congress and the people of the United States, we would all be in Siberia by now." The responsibility which we bear is an enormous one — and it is particularly acute for Christians, who can assert that these fundamental moral issues transcend any one religion or people. At the Second World Conference on Soviet Jewry in Brussels, Belgium, earlier this year, all Christians present issued a "Call to Christian Conscience," asserting that "this generation of Christians will not be silent as we raise our voices in support of the struggle to prevent the cultural and spiritual annihilation of the Jews of the Soviet Union.... We call upon the Soviet Union to implement those provisions of the Helsinki Agreement which relate to freedom of thought, conscience, religion, and belief, and to the right to emigrate.... We cannot remain silent or indifferent in the face of the continuing grave and dehumanizing injustices that have been inflicted upon the Jews and other groups in the Soviet Union."

Now, as the validity of the Helsinki Agreement remains to be determined, perhaps largely by the events of the coming year, none of us can remain indifferent. If we do all we can this year to encourage compliance, perhaps eventually we will witness the fulfillment of the biblical promise which concludes the Brussels Conference Call to Christian Conscience: "To open the eyes of the blind, to bring prisoners out from confinement, and from the dungeon, those who live in darkness" (Isa 42:7).

Chapter 43

Soviet Jews Suffer Mounting Repression

Will the advent of Yuri Andropov as the new Soviet leader and the deterioration of relations between the White House and the Kremlin mean the termination of the remarkable exodus of 270,000 Soviet Jews over the past dozen years? That was the difficult question confronted by 2,000 Jews and 50 Christians from 31 nations at the Third World Conference on Soviet Jewry held in Jerusalem March 15-17.

The fact is, no one knows what is ahead for the 3 million Jews in the Soviet Union. What is clear is that their condition has worsened. Emigration in 1982 declined to 2,400 from a high of 51,000 in 1979. Harassment has intensified and discrimination against the estimated 200,000 refuseniks has become more severe than ever before.

The delegates in Jerusalem were clearly frightened. But they kept encouraging each other that the miracles they helped to bring about because of the First and Second World Conferences on Soviet Jewry in Brussels in 1971 and 1976 can be continued.

I was elated but also depressed at the events of the Jerusalem meeting. Anatoly Scharansky, the activist sentenced to 13 years for alleged spying for the United States, was my guide and translator in Moscow in August 1975. He took me to visit Andrei Sakharov and many other dissidents, several of whom I met in a reunion at the World Conference in Jerusalem. But I talked with them about those who after years of applying are still held in the land they want to leave. We also talked to

First published in the *The Christian Century*, May 18, 1983.

dozens of Israeli citizens who are intensely anxious that their close relatives be allowed to leave the Soviet Union and join them. Some 180,000 Soviet Jews have arrived in Israel since 1970. But in hundreds, even thousands of cases they have not been able to bring about the release of their spouses, parents or children from Russia.

I spoke with a 78-year-old woman, recently widowed, who has been begging since 1972 for her son and her grandchildren to be granted permission to join her in Israel. They applied years ago. As a result, the son, an engineer, lost his position and — in a Catch-22 situation — is now being prosecuted for being unemployed. This woman, like most of the 180,000 Soviet Jews now in Israel, feels that only worldwide pressure on the Kremlin will induce the U.S.S.R. to live up to the 1975 Helsinki Accords, which it signed and which guarantee the right to emigrate for the purpose of reunification of families.

Anti-Semitism in the Soviet Union has long been ferocious. The pogroms and the persecutions there were two of the major causes that produced political Zionism. For a short period after 1917, the Russian Jewish community — which still accounts for 20 per cent of all of the Jews in the world — was treated with toleration. But since around 1920 the suppression of Judaism has been an objective of every regime — in particular, of Stalin's. Synagogues that numbered 3,000 in 1917 are now reduced to 40 at most. The destruction of Yiddish culture and the Hebrew language have been goals ruthlessly pursued. The examples of anti-Semitic and anti-Zionist literature that were on display at the Jerusalem Conference were simply unbelievable.

Panels of jurors, scientists and churchmen at the Jerusalem Conference examined the persistence of anti-Semitism in Soviet society. Lawyers recounted their efforts (filing briefs, bringing cases to international forums) to point out the gross violations of internationally recognized human rights in which Soviet officials engage. A new international association of lawyers devoted to the legal rights of Soviet Jews emerged from the Jerusalem meeting. Scientists spoke of their scientific colleagues in the U.S.S.R. who, like Dr. Alexander Lerner in Moscow, have lost professorships because they applied to make "aliyah." Scientists also brought out the fact that Jewish young people are being denied admission to the universities of Russia. In 1968-69 Jewish students enrolled in higher education in the Soviet Union totaled 111,900. In 1976-77 (the last year of published data) that number had declined to 66,900.

The church-related spokespeople at the Jerusalem Conference related their activities around the world on behalf of Soviet Jews. The great struggle for Jewish liberation in the Soviet Union is being waged with only the slightest support from Christians, many of whom are engaged in the work of Amnesty International and other world human rights groups.

One active ecumenical group is the Interreligious Task Force for Soviet Jewry, established in 1972 by Christian and Jewish leaders in the United States. With Sister Ann Gillen as its executive director, this unit sends delegates to the meetings of the Helsinki nations in Belgrade and Madrid and disseminates information about refuseniks and related issues in the U.S.S.R. At the Jerusalem meeting this task force emerged as clearly the best organized of all of the Christian organizations seeking to sensitize the world to the harsh conditions imposed on the Jews of Russia. The church people from the Netherlands could also point to impressive accomplishments. But one would have to conclude that, generally speaking, Christians around the world are unaware of or are silent about the severity of the repression of Soviet Jews. One is reminded of the silence of Christians during the Holocaust.

One Christian group received mixed reviews in Jerusalem — the International Christian Embassy, an evangelical group based in Israel and financed in part by the religious right wing in America. Based on some of the concepts about Israel favored by the Moral Majority, the ICE is welcomed by some conservative elements in Israel but is viewed with some suspicion by the mainline Christian bodies.

A handful of Christian clergy in the United States has been devoted to Soviet Jews. One is John Steinbruck of Luther Place Church in Washington, D.C. For many years he has preached about what the establishment of the state of Israel should mean to Christians. He has visited the refuseniks in Russia.

There are some indications that a Christian protest movement might be developing, but they are slender. One church-related college in the United States is going to give an honorary degree in absentia this year to Alexander Piritsky, one of the best-known refuseniks. A group of Catholic nuns in the recent past fasted to express their solidarity with Scharansky. Cardinal Joseph Bernardin recently made a statement on Soviet Jews and pleaded for Scharansky.

But the Jews at the Jerusalem Conference said that Soviet Jews feel they are alone. They have the deepest apprehension about what Andropov might do. As the head of the KGB, he was one of the leaders in the actions to suppress all vestiges of the Jewish religion in the U.S.S.R. The level of angst at the Jerusalem Conference seemed to rise by the hour as the full implications of what is happening in Moscow, Lenningrad, Riga, Odessa and elsewhere unfolded. What if all emigration were terminated? Will the Kremlin seek a "final solution" for Judaism and even for the Jews? Should the techniques and tactics of the Jewish community — so successful from 1970 to 1980 — be altered, since they are not producing results now? What are the alternatives? One of the few items that drew consensus was the conviction that "noise" — petitions, demonstrations, resolutions and statements by churches — must continue and escalate.

There was also consensus among the 2,000 delegates, 525 of them from the United States, that the Soviet Union has to be denounced. Prime Minister Menachem Begin reminisced at the conference about his time in a Soviet jail, confined because of his pro-Zionist activities. Even Israel's former foreign minister, Abba Eban, engaged in hard rhetoric about the lawlessness of Soviet leaders. The word "detente" was not heard in Jerusalem. Delegates' anger at the cruelty and inhumanity of the Kremlin toward Jews undoubtedly blocked any enthusiasm for such rapprochement.

But it was Abba Eban who pointed out that the highest levels of Jewish emigration occurred during periods of East-West accomodation. Abba Eban did not, however, urge that the delegates endorse detente in some form; he urged them not to sit in judgment on the postures of the superpowers, lest this hurt their cause. But everyone knew that he was speaking about Ronald Reagan when he said that "rhetorical violence and strategic confrontation" are not productive.

One sometimes had the feeling at Jerusalem that although the Jewish leaders must continue to voice their anger and anguish at the Kremlin, perhaps nothing will improve the chances of substantial emigration. The Helsinki Accords consist of three parts: military accommodations, economic adjustments and the observance of human rights. Can the Soviets be expected to observe the part on human rights if they feel that the United States is violating the letter or the spirit of the first two parts of the agreements?

There may well be other causes for the radical change in the Politburo's policy on emigration — a 95 per cent decline in permitted departures. One is the displeasure of the Kremlin at the fact that around 60 per cent of Jewish emigres in recent months have gone not to Israel but to the United States or elsewhere. Invitations to these people come from Israel from relatives interested in family reunification. Soviet officials are obviously resentful of the fact that emigres with highly developed skills go to the United States rather than Israel. Jewish spokespeople counter that when Soviet Jews arrive in Vienna for processing, they are stateless people who may, under international law, go to any country that will receive them. At the Jerusalem Conference there was some talk of asking Moscow to help to arrange for direct flights to Israel from the Soviet Union, with the question of any further moves to be settled at a later time.

A third possible reason for the radical decline in emigration was hinted at but not openly discussed in Jerusalem. It is the possibility that the Soviet officials are tired of being bothered by demonstrations and propaganda concerning Soviet Jewry around the world and that they have now determined to eliminate the problem by eliminating the Jewish religion in Russia. The U.S.S.R. has done everything theoretically necessary to obliterate Jewish language and culture. Yet it endures and even flowers. It is conceivable that the Kremlin could decree the elimination of the word "Jew" on the identity cards of the 3 million people whose parents were Jewish. But to what nationality could the Soviet officials assign the Jews?

Regardless of the reasons for the present cutoff in emigration, the Jewish community around the world is determined to make it possible for every Soviet Jew to emigrate. The spectacular liberation of 280,000 since 1970 argues that it can be done. The delegates in Jerusalem would not listen to counterarguments. They recalled that Theodore Herzl, the founder of Zionism, frequently said that one of the fundamental purposes for the establishment of Israel was to form a homeland for the Jews of Russia. Israel is ready; indeed, it needs all the immigrants it can get.

The Jews who came to the Jerusalem Conference had many questions about the policies of the Begin government. Many Jews were troubled about the invasion of Lebanon — particularly the shelling and occupation of Beirut.

But all these questions were displaced as the avalanche of information and horror stories about Soviet Jews gained momentum. Diaspora Jews and Israelis are deeply divided about Begin's militarism and his territorial claims to Judea and Samaria. But on the plight of Soviet Jews they are completely united, as the potential (or predictable) tragedies of the Andropov era unfold.

It is impossible to predict the fate of the 400,000 Soviet Jews who have received invitations to immigrate from individual Israeli hosts. Will they withdraw their applications to leave, as some are now being asked to do by Soviet authorities? Could the whole movement to leave the Soviet Union dry up if the consequences of applying are made even more draconian? Or will the Soviets, tired of all the controversy, finally respond to a Moses-like demand to "let my people go"?

What could the Christian role in this possible exodus be? I recalled the words spoken to me by Dr. Sakharov in his apartment in August 1975: "Only the Christians of America can liberate the Jews of Russia." If this is more than a rhetorical flourish, the Christians of America have a great deal to do. It may be that they feel grief and guilt over the record of anti-Semitism of the churches through the centuries.

Many of the Christians who came to the Jerusalem Conference have experienced that grief and guilt. A Catholic woman from Ecuador expressed her pain at the anti-Semitism which she sees in her church. A Baptist member of the Canadian

Parliament thrilled the Jerusalem assembly by his statements about why he will fight for the rights of Jewish dissidents. And an Anglican woman from Scotland told me that she feels constant shame because of the way that Christians have treated Jews.

Such sentiments are not very visible in Christian pronouncements, however. And Jews do not appear to rely on them. They feel alone in their struggle for Israel against the Arab nations and at the United Nations, where in 1975, 72 nations voted in favor of the proposition that Zionism is a form of racism.

The final declaration of the Jerusalem Conference was a vigorous, even vehement plea to the Kremlin to reopen its gates, end the persecution of Jews and stop its global dissemination of anti-Semitic literature. The statement opens by proclaiming that the Jews at the Third World Conference on Soviet Jewry are "joined by Christian leaders." It would indeed be beautiful if history recorded that in the late 1980s the Christians of the world joined together to bring about the deliverance from the Soviet Union of some 3 million believers in the God of Abraham, Isaac and Jacob.

APPENDIXES

The Impeachment
of
President Nixon

Resolution of Impeachment of President Nixon

Mr. Speaker, with great reluctance I have come to the conclusion that the House of Representatives should initiate impeachment proceedings against the president. My mind has resisted that conclusion for many months. I have now, however, come to the point where I must follow my convictions and my conscience and recommend that the House of Representatives pursue its duty under article 2, section 4 of the Constitution which provides for the impeachment of the president.

Before discussing the historical, constitutional, and legal justification for my conclusion I think that it is appropriate to note that the recent revelation which persuaded me that I could no longer be silent on this point was the recent disclosure that President Nixon conducted a totally secret air war in Cambodia for 14 months prior to April 30, 1970. On that day President Nixon announced to the Nation that he had ordered American ground forces to enter Cambodia. The President stated to the Nation that in the 5 years prior to April 30, 1970, the United States had "scrupulously" observed the neutrality of Cambodia. The President made this statement with the full knowledge that he had personally ordered thousands of B-52 air raids over Cambodia during the 14 months prior to America's invasion on the ground of neutral Cambodia.

It is appropriate to discuss the following issues:

First published in the *Congressional Record*, July 31, 1973.

First. An impeachment cannot be substituted for either a vote of no confidence or an indictment for criminal offenses.

Second. The activities and omissions of President Nixon add up to conduct which merits impeachment by the House of Representatives.

Third. A hearing on impeachment by the House of Representatives is the only possible way by which the questions of the citizens of America can be answered and their confidence in government restored.

1. What Activities or Omissions Amount to Impeachable Conduct?

All of the literature concerning the Constitutional Convention demonstrates that there is no evidence that any member of that convention expressed the opinion that impeachment was only intended to cover indictable offenses. That is the conclusion of the learned volume by Professor Raoul Berger entitled *Impeachment: The Constitutional Problems* —Harvard University Press, 1973. Professor Berger states that:

> One may fairly conclude that indictability was not the test of impeachment....

The same author expands on this by asserting:

> In sum, "high crimes and misdemeanors" without roots in the ordinary criminal law and which, as far as I could discover, had no relation to whether an indictment would lie in the particular circumstances. (Berger, 62.)

The House of Representatives, therefore, should not wait before commencing impeachment proceedings until some clear indictable offense on the part of the president becomes manifest. The Constitution makes it clear that the founding fathers separated impeachment from subsequent criminal prosecution. The words "high crimes and misdemeanors" do not presuppose conduct punishable by the general criminal law.

The report of the House Judiciary Committee recommending the impeachment of Judge English in 1926 was clear on this point:

> ... Although frequently debated, and the negative advocated by some high authorities, it is now, we believe, considered that impeachment is not confined alone to acts which are forbidden by the constitution or Federal statutes. The better sustained and modern view is that the provision for impeachment in the constitution applied not only to high crimes and misdemeanors as those words were understood in Common Law but also acts which are not defined as criminal and made subject to indictment, and also to those which affect the public welfare. (H. Rept. 653, 69th Congress, 1st Session, page 9-10.)

Indeed it is uncertain whether the constitutional provisions for impeachment set up a criminal proceeding at all. To be sure the impeachment provisions seem to point in the direction of criminality because they employ the language of the criminal law. At the same time article 3, section 2(3) of the Constitution provides that:

> The trial of all crimes, except in cases of impeachment, shall be by jury.

Similarly article 2, section 2(1) empowers the President to grant "pardon for offenses against the United States, except in cases of impeachment." It is also significant that article 1, section 3(7) distinguishes very clearly removal from office from the subsequent punishment which can be received after indictment.

Impeachment, therefore, should not be looked upon or compared with an indictment nor should the role of the House of Representatives in considering the impeachment of a president be deemed to be that of a grand jury. Perhaps the best definition of impeachment is taken from the classic work on jurisprudence of Justice Story. This classical source states that impeachment is:

> "... proceeding purely of a political nature. It is not so much designed to punish an offender as to secure the state

against gross official misdemeanors. It touches neither his
person nor his property, but simply divests him of his political capacity."

Impeachment is a noncriminal and nonpenal proceeding.
Impeachment proceedings do not permit the person subject to
them to claim double jeopardy if, in fact, he is tried for a crime
subsequent to the impeachment.

From my review of virtually every legal and constitutional
treatise ever written in American history on impeachment the
term "removal from office" could be used as a synonym for
"impeachment." Professor Berger notes in his definitive study
of impeachment that the framers of the Constitution made
clear the noncriminal aspects of the impeachment process but
that:

> A thorough-going attempt to clarify the non-penal aspect
> of removal would have required the framers to coin a fresh
> and different vocabulary — perhaps an insuperable task in
> all the circumstances.

The framers of the Constitution were steeped in English
history. They feared that the executive branch of government
might be transformed into a monarchy. At the same time the
authors of the Constitution desired to perpetuate the independence of the executive branch of government. In order to maintain a system of checks against the executive, while not really
threatening the independence of that branch of government,
the framers of the Constitution provided for impeachment
which, it could be argued, is a narrow exception to the separation of powers.

The history of the Constitutional Convention makes it clear
that, in debating impeachment, the framers were almost totally
concerned with the powers of the President. The inclusion of
the "Vice President and all civil officers," now in the Constitution, was not added until shortly before the convention
adjourned.

Studies of the process by which the Constitution was written
make clear that the framers furnished to the House of Representatives a norm for impeachment. That norm, adopted from

English law, stated that impeachment can arise from a serious failing even though such conduct or failure to act would not be under English law an indictable, common law crime. At the same time the framers of the Constitution withheld from Congress the power to inflict criminal punishment. The framers adopted the words "high crimes and misdemeanors" because they knew that these words had a limited and technical meaning.

The framers of the Constitution clearly understood the potential abuse of the power of impeachment which it conferred on the House of Representatives. They understood that impeachment could become a very partisan weapon and that its existence could threaten presidential independence. Nonetheless they chose to give to the House of Representatives the power of impeachment as a curb on presidential conduct which would be less than criminal but more than tolerable.

I have reluctantly come to the conclusion that a hearing on the impeachment of the president is indicated.

II. Does President Nixon's Conduct Justify Impeachment?

In view of the fact that the Members of the House of Representatives act under the Constitution as the triers of fact in any impeachment proceedings it is not appropriate to set forth circumstances surrounding recent events in a way to suggest that the only possible inference from these circumstances is a conclusion that justifies impeachment. Consequently I raise questions that in my judgment the House should seek to answer. The list of questions is by no means complete or comprehensive. Nor is it appropriate to suggest that these questions will be resolved by the Senate Watergate Committee. Indeed, one can argue, based upon the questions asked by the Senate Watergate Committee, that the members of that panel may well be usurping the right to investigate the possibility of impeachment — a right granted by the Constitution exclusively to the House of Representatives.

The questions to which the House, in an impeachment proceeding, should address itself include the following:

First. Was there any justification for President Nixon authorizing 3,630 air strikes over Cambodia between March 1969 and May 1970? This period of 14 months of intensive bombing cost $140 million. Since the Congress knew nothing of the secret raids in Cambodia was this money obtained from the Congress under "false premises" and spent in an unconstitutional manner?

Was the president, furthermore, truthful with the American people when he stated to them on April 30, 1970, that "for 5 years neither the United States nor South Vietnam has moved against enemy sanctuaries — in Cambodia — because we did not wish to violate the territory of a neutral nation"?

Did the president, moreover, acquiesce in wrongdoing when the National Security Council, headed by Henry Kissinger, ordered the falsification of military records in order to prevent disclosure of the clandestine air war on Cambodia?

Second. Were impeachable offenses committed by the president in connection with the taping of all conversations which he made on the phone and all conversations that took place in various parts of the White House? If Mr. John Ehrlichman is accurate when he stated that he talked with Mr. L. Patrick Gray, then Director of the FBI, from a phone in the President's office it was a clear violation of federal law since a phone was tapped without the permission of the sender or the receiver of the message.

Once again the answers to those questions with respect to the tapes may or may not be revealed in the Senate Watergate proceedings. But the House of Representatives is nonetheless not absolved from its obligation to investigate this matter insofar as it pertains to the question of impeachment — a subject over which the House has exclusive jurisdiction under the Constitution.

Third. Every court that has ruled on the question of impoundment has decided against the administration. Nonetheless the impounding goes on. It was revealed on July 26, 1973 that the Secretary of Health, Education, and Welfare had withheld $1.1 billion over the past year in moneys authorized for major federal health programs. By what right does a Federal agency refuse to spend more than a fifth of all of the expenditures appropriated by the Congress for the health services budget? Affected by this refusal to spend were federal mental health programs, the National Heart and Lung Institute, and the National Cancer Institute — the last having been given priority by the president himself.

Fourth. The establishment of a super-secret security force within the White House itself is, of course, unprecedented in all of American history. The assumption by the president of the statutory tasks of the FBI and the CIA raises the most serious questions concerning the impeachment of a chief executive who in effect established a national police force accountable only to himself.

There are many other questions that could be raised concerning the legality, the constitutionality and the propriety of action and inaction by President Nixon.

III. Conclusions and Recommendations

Until the last few days I, like other members of the House of Representatives, took refuge in the hope that somehow these questions would be resolved either in the courts or in the Senate Watergate Committee hearings. I am persuaded that members of the House can no longer entertain such hopes. The legality of the conduct of the several dismissed top aides to the president may or may not be fully resolved by the Senate hearings or in the courts. But the question of the impeachment of the president can be resolved in no other place but the House of Representatives.

It will no longer do for members of the House of Representatives to suggest that no serious question exists. Reliable national polls indicate that some 70 percent of the American people feel that the president was involved in some way in the coverup of the Watergate scandals. Almost one-fourth of the people in the Nation have expressed the opinion that the President should be removed from office.

If the House of Representatives is to be truly the house of the people we can no longer tell almost one-fourth of America's citizens that they must expect the Senate or the courts to determine whether or not the president has committed impeachable offenses. The determination of that question is a right and duty which the House has under the Constitution and a duty which the House may not delegate to any other body in America.

Months ago the House Committee on Banking and Currency had a vote as to whether they would investigate the then emerging scandals related to the Watergate. The committee in a closely divided vote decided not to investigate those activities at that time.

I think that the time has arrived when the members of the House must seek to think the unthinkable and to search diligently into our convictions and our conscience and decide what is our duty under the Constitution as we behold the unprecedented revelations which everyday become more incredible.

Not a few observers and students of the House of Representatives have stated that they feel that the House has been too timid in asserting its constitutional powers with respect to a declaration of war. Many commentators have also indicated that the House of Representatives has not been vigorous enough in the exercise of its oversight function with respect to federal regulatory agencies, including the military. Many publicists, furthermore, have given their opinion that the House of Representatives not infrequently allows the Senate to erode the powers of the House.

I raise that central question with regard to the Senate Watergate proceedings. If the president is impeached by the House the members of the Senate must sit as the jury of the impeachment sent to the Senate by the House. Inevitably, therefore, the members of the Senate cannot and should not inquire into the existence of impeachable offenses on the part of the president. That role belongs exclusively to the House. I hope that the House of Representatives will overcome its understandable reluctance and confront the unpleasant but unavoidable fact that hearings on the impeachment of the president have now become our constitutional duty.

Finally, members of the House of Representatives should recognize that under the Constitution a proceeding with respect to his impeachment is the only way by which a president can vindicate himself. Colonel George Mason made this point when he addressed the framers of the constitution meeting in Philadelphia. Colonel Mason recommended that the constitution provide "for the regular punishment of the executive when his misconduct should deserve it." But Colonel Mason went on to state that the same procedure will provide for his honorable acquittal when he should be unjustly accused." For members of both political parties, therefore, the impeachment process should be looked upon as the one way by which the executive will be removed from office or by which he will secure that "honorable acquittal" to which he is entitled if he has been "unjustly accused."

Impeachment should not be a partisan issue. Impeachment should be a question which Members of both political parties in the House of Representatives should be able to discuss. Nothing can be gained by denying the existence of this question and a great deal may be lost.

The one instance in which the House impeached a president — that of President Andrew Johnson in 1868 — was in all probability a gross abuse of the impeachment process and an attempt to penalize the President for differing with the policy of the Congress. If impeachment is to become a real issue within this House every member should resolve to avoid the excesses which stigmatized the impeachment proceedings a century ago. A decent regard for the design of the founders of our Constitution suggests that all of the members of Congress speak rationally, responsibly, and reasonably about those processes which we should discuss and develop if on the one hand we are to avoid the great mistakes which this House made a century ago and, on the other hand, we are to confront without blinking the fact that we alone as Members of the House have under the Constitution the duty to exercise the awesome power to impeach the president.

Nixon Bombing Defense Inadequate

In the statement which I submitted on July 31 justifying the resolution of impeachment of the president, I pointed to the secrecy of the bombing in Cambodia as a clearly impeachable offense. In his press conference at San Clemente, President Nixon pretended that he had resolved this problem in his August 20 address in New Orleans to the Veterans of Foreign Wars. The justification attempted in that talk of the secrecy of the 3630 air raids during 14 months in Cambodia is inadequate on several counts.

The president stated that the United States was under "no moral obligation to respect the sham" of the neutrality of Cambodia occupied by the North Vietnamese. The president clearly concedes that the United States was under a legal obligation not to bomb a neutral nation.

The president's allegation that the "enemy-occupied sanctuaries" of Cambodia "were no more neutral . . . than was northern France or Belgium in the late spring of 1944 when those territories were occupied by the Germans" is obviously false. France and Belgium were our allies in a war declared by the US against Germany while Cambodia has always been neutral and is not even a member of SEATO.

The fact that allegedly the "Cambodian government did not object to the strikes" cannot justify the first military assault in American history on a neutral nation with which America is at peace. Title 18 of the US Code specifically forbids such an

First published in the *National Catholic Reporter*, October 19, 1973.

assault. In addition, Prince Sihanouk has on several occasions after August 20 expressly denied that he ever agreed to the bombing.

The president states, furthermore, that he informed "appropriate congressional leaders" of the bombings. In a matter of this gravity there is no such thing as an "appropriate" congressional leader. The president has no constitutional or statutory right of any nature to give information to selected congressional leaders. Any practice to the contrary violates my right as a member of Congress and the rights of the 474,000 citizens I represent. If classified information is to be given to Congress all 535 members should be given (or denied) that security clearance which is granted, when necessary, even to the GS-4 typist.

The president, seeming to recognize his vulnerability because of his action in launching an air war without telling the American people, states that "there was *no* secrecy as far as the government leaders were concerned who had any *right* to know or *need* to know" (emphasis supplied).

Can a very few congressional "leaders" (a title acquired by sheer seniority and not by any selection by the members of Congress or the people) have any "right" or "need" to know about a secret war costing at least $140,000,000 which is greater than the identical "right" and "need" of all 535 members of Congress? The answer has to be "no."

The most outrageous contentions made by Nixon to justify 14 months of secret bombing rest on his assertion that "had we announced the air strikes, the Cambodian government would have been compelled to protest" and "the bombing would have had to stop." This shocking double standard evokes two comments:

Cambodia would have been "compelled" to protest, we are told, because that nation is and must continue to be a neutral country. If Cambodia asserted this neutral status the United States, Nixon tells us, would have been required to recognize the truth and stop the bombing! The US, in other words, will bomb a neutral nation until or unless that nation protests and proclaims its neutrality before the court of world opinion. In admitting to this incredible way of acting, Nixon concedes that the US would not air bomb a neutral nation — even to save the lives of American soldiers in South Vietnam — if that nation asserted its neutrality as a shield against our B 52s!

Mr. Nixon claims that Prince Sihanouk invited him to visit Cambodia during the first spring of the bombings. The president claims this as evidence of approval by Sihanouk of the bombings. If, however, the head of the Cambodian government is this friendly why would a public protest by him of the bombings — a protest which would have allegedly been inevitable if the U.S. made public the air raids — have compelled the U.S. to stop the strikes? It would not be the point of international law raised by Sihanouk but, to be blunt, by American public opinion.

Mr. Nixon has elaborated hypotheses and premises to justify his secrecy about his ecalation of the war into Cambodia eight weeks after he became president. All that he says, and implies, points to the unavoidable conclusion that he conducted the air war over Cambodia in secrecy because he was afraid — or he knew — that American public opinion would not tolerate it.

Such deception, in my judgment, is an impeachable offense.

Analyzing Watergate Issues

Mr. Speaker, a large number of proposals have been advanced in the wake of President Ford's pardon of Richard Nixon. Many of these proposals are interwoven and go back to the central fact that former President Nixon aborted the impeachment process by his resignation.

I would like to furnish accurate information and some judgment on the major questions and proposals which are now emerging. My comments will relate to: First, the pardon of Richard Nixon and other prospective Watergate pardons; second, the proposed $850,000 for Richard Nixon; third, methods proposed to guarantee the right of the American public to know the full details about Watergate; fourth, proposals to alter or amend the power to pardon given in the Constitution to the president; and fifth, related proposals concerning the 25th Amendment.

The Pardon of Richard Nixon

President Ford's decision to grant an absolute pardon to Richard Nixon is constitutionally and morally wrong. It cannot be justified by any reading of the spirit and intent of the Constitution nor can it be reconciled with the most fundamental moral assumptions underlying the administration of justice in America.

First published in the *Congressional Record*, September 24, 1974.

217

At the Constitutional Convention in 1787 a motion was made to restrict the grant of pardon only to cases "after conviction." This motion was withdrawn after the delegates were advised that a pardon before judgment might sometimes be necessary in order "to obtain the testimony of accomplices in a crime." It seems clear, therefore, that President Ford exceeded any power conferred by the framers of the Constitution with respect to preindictment pardons.

President Ford's action is also open to question on another constitutional point. The Constitution withholds the power to pardon from a President in "cases of impeachment." The intent of the framers was to prevent presidents from doing what Gerald Ford has done, using the pardoning power to rehabilitate political allies whose conduct merited impeachment. If Richard Nixon had taken his chances on conviction in the Senate after impeachment in the House and had lost, President Ford would be expressly barred by the Constitution itself from ever pardoning Nixon. Is it proper or just to ignore and flaunt the manifest intent of the Constitution by taking advantage of the technicality that Nixon resigned rather than allow himself to be removed by impeachment?

President Ford acknowledged that:

> There are no historic or legal precedents to which I can turn in this matter. . . .

Nevertheless he moves forward with the amazing and unbelievable assertion that:

> Only I, as President, have the constitutional power to firmly shut and seal this book (of Watergate).

What the President forgets is that the last chapters of that book have not yet been written and that his gratuitous assumptions convey the inevitable impression that he does not want those chapters to be written or read.

The Constitution may be vague on the contours of a president's right to pardon. But English history, basic logic, and language itself all teach us that a pardon cannot be applied to acts of wrongdoing that have never been proved, admitted, or even alleged. To extend a pardon to such a wide range of unnamed, unnumbered, and indeed unknown events is more of a coverup than a reprieval.

No matter how compassionate one tries to be in assessing the pardon given to Richard Nixon one cannot escape the conclusion that Mr. Ford has told us that a president may ignore the laws and the Constitution, evade an impeachment inquiry, lie to the Congress and the country, and still obtain a pardon from his successor.

President Ford in his address on September 8 stated:

> I deeply believe in equal justice, for all Americans, whatever their station or former station. The law, whether human or divine, is no respecter of persons. . . .

But then he adds that "the law is a respecter of reality." Apparently in this case, Mr. Ford is telling us, "reality" means that we cannot have "equality."

President Ford's incoherent statement speaks of compassion, but where is his compassion for the Constitution and the government of laws and not of men which was almost destroyed by some 30 lawless men acting at the direction of the nation's chief executive? Where is his compassion for the families of those already convicted or about to go on trial? Was he without compassion when he stated on August 28 that it would be "unwise and untimely for me" to act until some "legal process has been undertaken?"

When all the confusion is removed from President Ford's case he is really telling us that he does not want to see Mr. Nixon twisting slowly, slowly in the wind. Ford wants to protect us against ugly passions and bad dreams. Such contentions bring us back to the verbal illusions of Ron Ziegler and the absurd claims of President Nixon.

President Ford has placed the peace of mind of Richard Nixon above the peace of mind of the nation. He has divided the nation in ways which even the Saturday night massacre did not achieve. Indeed even Ford's designate vice president is now involved in the revival of the Watergate coverup. Rockefeller has said that Mr. Ford's pardon was an act of "conscience, compassion and courage." Those are words which make him already tarnished.

Americans want their government to be open and moral. Watergate has humiliated the people of this nation more than any previous scandal in all of American history. Americans are now humiliated once again by a president they never elected pardoning a former president whom they in effect impeached.

Several proposals have been made with respect to the pardon offered by President Ford to Richard Nixon. On September 12, for example, by a vote of 55 to 24, the Senate passed a resolution that there should be no more Watergate pardons until indictments and trials are over. This is merely a sense of the Congress resolution which, even if it were adopted by the House, has no binding effect upon the president. I am not certain that Congress has the authority to impede the constitutional power of the president to grant pardons.

Proposals have been made that the House Judiciary Committee investigate the circumstances surrounding the pardon granted to Richard Nixon by President Ford. While the intent of these resolutions is laudable, I am doubtful that Congress would find much documentation explaining why President Ford pardoned Mr. Nixon. It may be that the legality of the pardon itself will be tested in court in the near future. In any event, the Constitution does not require the president to disclose any reasons for the exercise of his power to grant reprieves and pardons.

I shall continue to follow very closely all of the developments related to the extraordinary pardon offered by the president in an extraordinary way to Mr. Nixon. I will continue to explore every method by which the fullest explanation can be ascertained.

Proposed Funds for Mr. Nixon

Sixteen years ago the Congress legislated that every "former president" who is not impeached would get $60,000 annual pension for life and up to $96,000 annually for staff expenses.

The Congress supplemented this 1958 statute by enacting in 1963 authorization for "transitional expenses" for former presidents. I must say that I am opposed to any "transitional expenses" for former presidents. I intend to vote against any federal funds for Richard Nixon except the pension to which he contributed as a member of Congress. I do this without any sense of vindictiveness but simply from reading the relevant statutes. It is clear to me that Congress intended to give pensions and other benefits only to presidents who served "honorably." Mr. Nixon, who resigned in order to avoid inevitable impeachment, does not fulfill that requirement.

Several proposals have emerged to amend the statutes concerning benefits for former presidents. At first I thought that we should tighten up existing legislation so that no future president could receive federal funds even though his presidency had been less than honorable. On second thought, however, I have come to the conclusion that all of the statutes awarding any federal funds to a former president should be totally reexamined. It may well be that such benefits are a part of the "imperial presidency" from which the nation has suffered so much. No one wants a former president to live in penury. At the same time, I cannot justify existing law which rewards any person who has held the presidency for any period, however brief, by a lifetime pension equal to the salary of a cabinet member or, at the present time, $60,000 per year.

Guaranteeing the Right of the American Public to Know All of the Facts About Watergate

Senator Mansfield has proposed that the president provide the American public full access to the tapes and other documents except in those rare instances where there is involved a clear case of national security. The Mansfield resolution also recommends that the president shoud assure the public full access to any information acquired during the Watergate investigations.

I have proposed a similar measure in the House except that the bill which I have sponsored would make it mandatory on the president to vindicate the right of the American people to know the whole truth about the Watergate scandal.

Of the hundreds of letters which I have received following the pardon of Mr. Nixon, many have urged that the impeachment proceedings be reopened by the House Judiciary Committee. While I continue to explore every possible reason for reopening the impeachment inquiry, it is my judgment at this time that the conclusion of this inquiry in the House and the Senate could result only in the disqualification of Mr. Nixon from holding any further public office. It appears to me that the use of a constitutional weapon like impeachment as a vehicle to bring out further facts about Watergate is a misuse of this constitutional device.

The Congress can direct the Special Watergate Prosecutor to include in his final report all information he has concerning Mr. Nixon's involvement in Watergate. Mr. Jaworski apparently feels reluctant to assume this obligation. In any action by the Congress designed to bring out the full facts about Mr. Nixon's involvement in Watergate, the utmost care should be taken to prevent the Congress from assuming law enforcement powers which only the executive branch of the government possesses.

It is possible that President Ford will ultimately abolish the office of the Special Watergate Prosecutor. Mr. Ford might prefer to follow up on all possible prosecutions through the ordinary channels of the Department of Justice.

In such event, the Congress would obviously have to insist that complete justice be done and that all of the Watergate break-in and coverup be comprehensively investigated.

The arrangement worked out by President Ford by which the General Services Administration and Mr. Nixon have exclusive jurisdiction to the tapes over the next several years raises the possibility that this curcial documentary evidence may never come to light. While the transfer of these tapes to California has been postponed, the long-term agreement has not yet been revised.

I feel certain that the Congress, insofar as its jurisdiction permits, will seek to assert the rights of the people of America to due process with regard to disclosures from the tapes.

Some bills have been filed that would make all presidential documents the property of the US government. Certainly, a clarification of the law in this area would be desirable. I am in the process of perfecting a bill which will state that all public papers of federal elected officials belong to the people.

I feel obliged to reiterate, however, that the sense of Congress and any laws that may be enacted will be insufficient to compel the full revelation of all of the facts behind the Watergate scandal. Only the patience, the persistence, and the patriotism of vast numbers of American citizens will be sufficient to prevent a further extension of the coverup.

The Scope of the Pardoning Power of the President

Because of the most serious objections to the presidential pardon of Mr. Nixon, several members of Congress have proposed restrictions on the right of the president to grant pardons. These measures have ranged from a proposal that would require the president to provide Congress with a full report on the justification of all presidential pardons to a suggestion that the president be permitted to grant pardons before conviction only if a majority of both Houses of Congress concur.

The House Judiciary Committee will hold hearings as soon as feasible on these proposals. In view of the fact that the power to pardon possessed by all previous presidents has seldom if ever been abused, there must be the most serious and indeed overwhelming justification established before a constitutional amendment should be initiated.

Proposals to Alter the 25th Amendment

When two-thirds of the House and Senate and three-fourths of the states ratified the 25th Amendment in 1967, no one really contemplated the possibility of having both the president and the vice president elected, not by the people, but by the two branches of Congress. Because this undesirable situation may become reality in the near future, several persons have proposed that the Constitution be amended once again to provide for a popular election some 60 or 90 days after the vice presidency becomes vacant. This is, of course, precisely the practice followed by state law when a member of the US House of Representatives dies or resigns during his term of office. On the other hand, when a U.S. Senator ceases for any reason to hold office before his term has been finished, the governor of the particular state appoints a senator to fill out the unexpired term.

All of these proposals were, of course, fully explored in the extensive debate that preceded the enactment of the 25th Amendment. Under that amendment, the 535 members of the House and Senate conduct a "minielection" in which these individuals are the surrogates or spokespersons for their constituents. The 25th Amendment was never intended to be a method by which an incumbent president could appoint a member of his own party as the vice president and expect the Congress to rubber stamp his choice. One could argue that in the confirmation of Gerald Ford the Congress of the United States did not completely fulfill the objectives of the 25th Amendment. It was said in response that the popular mandate obtained by Mr. Nixon in November 1972 ws so overwhelming that the Congess should reflect it in its voting on the candidacy for vice president of Gerald Ford.

I would assume that Congress might well have a different approach in connection with the candidacy for vice president of Mr. Nelson Rockefeller. It is certain that Mr. Rockefeller will be questioned very closely concerning his attitudes toward issues related to Watergate and in particular to his support of President Ford's decision to pardon Richard Nixon.

Although a thorough reexamination of the 25th Amendment might be in order sometime in the future, I am of the opinion at this time that it would be premature to reopen the extensive national debate which culminated in the adoption of the 25th Amendment in 1967.

Every American had hoped, Mr. Speaker, that in the next 1,000 days as we prepare to celebrate the Bicentennial of this nation, we could have seen restored to the presidency and to all of our institutions that integrity and majesty given to them by the Constitution. But instead, another dark night is descending upon us as the president takes action which appears to be an assault on the very foundations of equality, justice, and the right of the people to know.

This is not the time for the American people to remain quiet. It was the 3 million telegrams and letters which American men and women sent to their congressional representatives after the Saturday night massacre that brought about the impeachment inquiry.

I have received and responded to hundreds of antipardon letters and have assured my constituents that I will develop and justify a firm and fair stance on the various Watergate-related issues which are still before the Congress and the country. These will be resolved in the most satisfactory manner only if the people of America continue to demand and obtain a government of the people, by the people, and for the people.

Watergate: A Sickness that Strengthened a Nation

I remember very distinctly the first moment when I heard about the Watergate burglary. I read about it in the *Washington Post* on Saturday morning June 17, 1972.

I found it impossible to believe that this was anything more than a "third rate burglary," as the White House characterized it. President Nixon was riding high. His trip four months earlier to Peking ended in triumph as did his 13-day visit to Moscow and Europe which had culminated in a spectacular address to a joint session of Congress on June 1, 1972.

The Democratic Convention in Miami was scheduled for mid-July. Would Nixon's Committee to Re-Elect the President (CREEP) order an illegal entry into the office of the Democratic National Committee? For weeks, even months, I thought that those who wanted to involve Nixon in the break-in of Watergate were paranoid and almost irrational. I recall conversing with and urging McGovern after his nomination that he desist from making statements that the Nixon White House was the most corrupt administration in American history.

The inherent implausibility of Nixon's being involved in the work of the five Watergate burglars makes me even today still incredulous at the words on the June 23, 1972, tape which reveal beyond a doubt that Nixon knew about the break-in from the beginning.

First published in the *Boston Herald American*, July 11, 1982.

I recall vividly my first feelings when I learned on August 5, 1974, of the "smoking pistol" — the June 23, 1972, tape. I had a deep sense of betrayal. As a member of the House Judiciary Committee I had lived with the impeachment question from the moment I filed the first resolution of impeachment on July 31, 1973 — not because of Watergate but because of the clandestine bombing of Cambodia.

I remember very clearly talking with my colleagues on the House Judiciary Committee moments after the revelation of the June 23 tape. One of them later told me that he was practically in shock during the four days from August 5, 1974, to Nixon's resignation. All of us felt lied to. I had never had that experience before either in public or in private life.

I found it incredible — then and now — that six days after the break-in Nixon was plotting the cover-up in the Oval Office and that, even more unbelievable, he would for 784 days continue to deny the very existence of the cover-up. I wonder if Richard Nixon has ever fully realized that it was his conduct alone that sent 25 men involved in Watergate to jail.

Many Europeans have never understood why Americans were so horrified at the attempt of the Nixon administration to cover up a burglary which, by anybody's standards, was foolish and ill-conceived. The point which non-Americans miss is that the Watergate scandal was not about money like the Teapot Dome affair. Watergate was in essence a plot to steal an election and the Nixon administration was so ashamed of such conduct that it perverted the processes of government in order to conceal its act of political surveillance and sabotage.

There is abroad at the moment an inclination to undervalue and even belittle the post-Watergate ethical standards mandated by the Congress. The fact that on the 20th or 50th anniversary of the Watergate burglary history may record that the elimination of massive private funding for presidential campaigns — a reform prompted by Watergate — saved the presidency from the almost scandalous escalation of private political action committees which are now quite literally trying to "buy" seats in the Congress. The 1976 and 1980 presidential elections, financed with public monies matching modest private contributions, were models of decency, openness and fairness.

Other post-Watergate reforms may be more important than is now realized. Legislation following the nation's worst political scandal curbed the FBI and the CIA and drastically altered the ethical standards imposed on public officials. The strenthening of the Freedom of Information Act, passed over the veto of President Ford, is also a result of the determination of Congress never to have another Watergate.

Did Congress succeed in establishing institutions that would prevent another Watergate? It is too early to tell but at least Congress, viewing the subversion of America brought about in the Watergate scandal by an imperial presidency, tried to enact checks and safeguards so that no matter how twisted by blind ambition a future president might be he will not be able to subvert the executive branch of government to his own political objectives. Perhaps more importantly the country has made another Watergate more difficult — hopefully impossible — by demanding that the public and the media require complete openness and total accountability of all public officials.

Watergate purified the soul of America. After a period of fright, then of humiliation, America was strengthened with a sense of pride that not even the leader of the free world could destroy freedom in America.

INDEX